THE
CATCH

ALSO BY ANNA CLARK

Making Australian History
Private Lives, Public History
History's Children
The History Wars

For children:
Explored!
Convicted!

THE
CATCH

ANNA CLARK

VINTAGE BOOKS
Australia

VINTAGE

UK | USA | Canada | Ireland | Australia
India | New Zealand | South Africa | China

Vintage is part of the Penguin Random House group of companies whose addresses can be found at global.penguinrandomhouse.com

Penguin
Random House
Australia

First published by National Library of Australia in 2017
This revised edition published by Vintage in 2023

Cover photograph courtesy of Mitchell Library, State Library of New South Wales
(*Fishing on the rocks at Bondi*, 28 December 1936)
Cover design by Adam Laszczuk © Penguin Random House Australia Pty Ltd
Typeset in 12/18 pt Baskerville by Midland Typesetters, Australia

Printed and bound in Australia by Griffin Press, an accredited
ISO AS/NZS 14001 Environmental Management Systems printer

A catalogue record for this book is available from the National Library of Australia

ISBN 978 1 76134 220 2

penguin.com.au

MIX
Paper | Supporting
responsible forestry
FSC® C018684

We at Penguin Random House Australia acknowledge that Aboriginal and Torres Strait Islander peoples are the Traditional Custodians and the first storytellers of the lands on which we live and work. We honour Aboriginal and Torres Strait Islander peoples' continuous connection to Country, waters, skies and communities. We celebrate Aboriginal and Torres Strait Islander stories, traditions and living cultures; and we pay our respects to Elders past and present.

For Gab, Axel and Olaf

CONTENTS

Chapter 6

AUTHOR'S NOTE

This book was written on the lands of the Gadigal people of the Eora Nation and the Djiringanj people of the Yuin Nation, who I would like to acknowledge as the Traditional Custodians and storytellers of their Country.

I pay my respects to Elders past and present, and celebrate all the histories, traditions and living cultures of Aboriginal and Torres Strait Islander peoples on this land. They are Australia's first fishers, and their stories and practices have shaped Australian fishing history, as well as offering important, generous guidance on sustainability.

I use the terms 'Indigenous' and 'Aboriginal' to refer to Australia's First Peoples, but not interchangeably: taking a cue from the Australian Institute of Aboriginal and Torres Strait Islander Studies (AIATSIS), I use 'Aboriginal' to describe

First Peoples across mainland Australia, 'Torres Strait Islander' to describe the unique peoples and cultures of that region, and 'Indigenous' when describing them both – as in Australia's Indigenous peoples. However, it's also important to note that some Aboriginal people prefer to use the term 'Indigenous' to describe themselves, while in many communities the use of more localised references such as 'Koorie', 'Murrie', 'Noongar' or 'Palawa' is preferred, or more specific Country or clan names, such as Dharug, Wurundjeri or Yolŋu. Just as there is huge diversity in the culture, Country and language of Australia's First Peoples, including fishing practices and stories, there is also diversity in forms of self-identity and expression.

Where possible, I have used Indigenous place and Country names. There are frequently alternative spellings – such as Gadigal/Cadigal, Gomeroi/Kamileroi – and spellings and boundaries of Indigenous names and places change over time. Furthermore, detailed information about Aboriginal clan boundaries is sometimes missing or contested, especially where the effects of colonisation have been felt most thoroughly (such as across south-eastern Australia). In the past, observations of Australia's First Peoples and cultures tended not to record their distinctiveness or diversity, employing universal (and now considered offensive) terms to describe people and cultures from particular places. Where possible, I have suggested the clan and nation in those observations, but also include the original source material in full, to show how colonial lenses saw and annotated Indigenous Australia. After all, that is also part of Australia's fishing history.

INTRODUCTION

'THE ENDURING PLEASURE OF THROWING IN A LINE'
AUSTRALIA'S LOVE AFFAIR WITH FISHING

When they shut their eyes and pause for a minute, fishers have a place they go to in their mind. A special place, a fishing place. Mine is called Paradise, but you won't find it on any map.

I can be anywhere – hanging out the washing, sitting in traffic, waiting at the bus stop – and this glorious daydream appears. When the sun catches the side of my face, I close my eyes and I'm there, standing on the water's edge at Paradise in the late afternoon.

Every school holidays my family would head south from Sydney to my grandparents' property on the New South Wales South Coast. After the long drive, we'd spill out of the car and I'd run to look at the tide. I still do. If it's low enough, I grab a nipper pump, a bucket and a rod, and dash along the dirt track that winds through the bush, across the sandy paddocks and down to the beach.

Coastal mahogany trees shelter this quiet spot from the breeze, and a bend in the estuary gives a beautiful view across the lake to Mumbulla Mountain. Walking onto the beach, an oblivious kingfisher flits between the branches above the water, while soldier crabs scramble to bury themselves in the sand. As the sun goes down and the mullet start to jump, everything is covered in a final film of warm, soft light.

This is my special place.

As a kid I used to go down to the beach after dinner and watch 'the men' (my grandfather, my dad and my uncles) spinning off the rocks, or bait-fishing in the estuary. When I wanted to learn, they had me casting lures across the paddocks before I was allowed to join them by the water. Then they showed me how to tie on hooks, how to pump nippers and, most importantly, how to be patient.

Now I go to that same beach with my kids, and we catch flathead and luderick, trevally and whiting. A mask and snorkel reveal more beauties below the water. Flounder, octopus and leatherjacket hide in the weeds. Rays cover themselves with sand and pretend they're not there. Sometimes a rogue kingfish or salmon makes it up the estuary and onto the fire if we're lucky.

We like to think of it as *our* little piece of paradise, but it isn't, of course.

The banks peel back to reveal deep, full middens. Shells and fish bones are scattered through the sandy soil like hundreds and thousands. Countless – literally countless – generations have been here before, camping in this protected cove. Like us, the Djiringanj grabbed a feed of oysters or mussels off the rocks, picked crabs out of their holes, and fished for bream, whiting and flatties. Some still use this place, fishing the same sunset tides that Ancestors did for thousands of years.

It isn't just history that foils the fantasy that this place is mine alone. Out on the lake, oyster leases fill the tidal flats and commercial fishers set their nets across the small channels at night. In the holidays, daytrippers drop their boats at the local ramp and troll or drift by as we sit on the banks under the shade, looking out across the cool, clear water.

Everyone who fishes here contributes to the pressures on this spot. Waves from boats increase erosion of the banks, nets decimate prime breeding fish, and our passion for throwing a line in cuts into the stocks of everything else. Yet we love to fish, and we love eating fish, so we keep coming back.

Many Australians have a fishing spot like this. It could be a corner of Sydney Harbour, where flathead hide in the seagrass and squid flirt with jigs under the pier. Or it might be a beach on K'gari-Fraser Island when the tailor are running, or an outer reef in Queensland. Maybe it's a river in the Top End that you visit during wet-season build-up, a sand flat in the Coorong filled with whiting, or a clifftop on the Western Australian coast.

These are our fishing places, and they hold our stories. They're sites filled with memories and history, as families pass on techniques and generations of keen observation, as well as fishy tales of amazing catches and near misses. For many people, these places are also vital for supplementing a family feed. No wonder they're special.

Sometimes they're also sites of conflict and contest. Battles between recreational and commercial fishing, the belated recognition of Indigenous fishing rights, and demands for regulation all overlay this history. The fickle pressures of catch numbers, quotas and market prices have also shaped the ways we fish.

It's estimated that around five million Australians fish recreationally, and the commercial and recreational fishing industries account for almost fifteen billion dollars annually. It's one of the nation's most popular pastimes.

In every coastal town, there's a bait shop and a boat ramp. In garages around the country, fishing rods are strung up waiting for the next holiday, or weekend, or tide. Fishing guides sell by the thousand. Meanwhile, lives and livelihoods continue to be made and lost on the back of commercial booms and busts.

All of this points to an ongoing passion for fish and fishing in Australia, which is complemented by a bevy of local tales (tall and true), government and industry reports, and commissioned histories. Fishing stories fill pages of myriad memoirs and untold hours of oral histories, describing the simple delights of watching the world go by from the tiller of a tinnie.

Our country's love of fishing is also backed up by serious research. In the most recent national survey of Australian recreational fishing, published in 2003, 37 per cent of respondents said they fished to relax and unwind, 15 per cent said they fished to be with family, and 13 per cent went fishing to be outdoors. In total, only 26 per cent said their primary motivation for catching fish was for sport or food. That means most people (65 per cent) said they fished not simply for the catch, but to be out there on the water. According to the Fisheries Research and Development Corporation, which is conducting an updated survey into recreational fishing in Australia, these figures are still current – you only have to look at boat sales during the COVID-19 pandemic to see how important fishing was to Australians in the midst of lockdown.While the thrill of the catch is undeniable, fishing is about so much more than bagging out with a great haul. For many, it's the smell of salt spray and the sound of the waves. Others think there's nothing better than picking sea lettuce off the rocks in pursuit of a winter luderick, or gathering cunjevoi or crabs to try to catch a thumping drummer or a bream.

We love the feeling of a lure being smashed. We dream about a favourite river bend, where the current and tangle of snags are just right for a perch or Murray cod. We love watching the tide turn or the sun set, knowing that the first bite or haul of the net is only minutes away.

That's because 'fishing largely consists of not catching fish', as the art historian (and avid fisho) Robert Hughes once mused in his book *A Jerk on One End: Reflections of a Mediocre Fisherman*. It's about operating at a different pace, about being in the world differently. 'To fish at all, even at a humble level, you must notice things: the movement of the water and its patterns, the rocks, the seaweed, the quiver of tiny scattering fish that betrays a bigger predator under them.'

This isn't the sort of knowledge you learn from school or from books, as the environmental historian Jodi Frawley explains. Instead, fishing is an 'embodied practice' that emphasises 'stillness, quietness and patience'. It's learned by doing, and by being in place – by sitting with grandparents on the jetty, or out with an Elder in a boat, or on the beach chatting away an afternoon with friends. Fishing knowledge is passed down through generations and connects us to the natural world. That's why our fishing stories of that special catch or place are so important.

But here's the real 'catch': a constant pressure on wild fish stocks comes from our appetite to hunt and consume them, in addition to the ecological pressures from industrial and agricultural development, as well as climate change.

Australia's fisheries are some of the most regulated in the world, with strict limits on how much can be taken, and with an increasingly sophisticated system to measure fish populations, as well as programs to restock them. Yet the pressures on our 'special' places are still very real.

Australia's waters were overfished for more than a century. Partly, those practices were based on scientific ignorance; there was little knowledge about the extent of our fisheries, which appeared abundant and limitless. Those earlier forms of commercial fishing also reflected particular understandings about the need (and even the national duty) to harness and harvest our natural resources. Australia's progress depended on it.

There were plenty of fish in the sea – until there weren't anymore.

Over time, increasing awareness about the precarious-
ness of Australia's fisheries changed the ways we managed
these places, and the ways we fished. Once, huge hauls gave us
bragging rights. Nowadays, you're just as likely to see a trophy
catch captured on Instagram before being released back into the
ocean to swim another day, or families fishing for their dinner,
but not to excess. Commercial fishers monitor and measure,
and stocks are regularly evaluated.

What's remained constant is our passion for 'the catch'.

This book explores Australia's love affair with fishing. It
traces the earliest known accounts of Indigenous fishing, as well
as those initial European encounters with Australia's waters. It
charts the development of the fishing industry, from its bountiful
but rudimentary beginnings to an era of increasing technology,
management and regulation. And it tells the story of Australian angling, which began with little more than pieces of string
tied to the end of some sticks but is now a multibillion-dollar
high-tech industry.

The Catch captures our fishing traditions, as well as changing
understandings of Australian fisheries. Most of all, it savours
the enduring pleasure of throwing in a line and waiting for that
tug on the end.

Within earshot of the water, a length of kangaroo tendon is tied around the first two joints of an infant girl's left little finger and tightened. The circulation cuts off, the flesh mortifies and eventually it falls away. The tiny, blackened digit is taken out into the water and dropped to the fish below.

CHAPTER 1

'SOME UNERRING INSTINCT'
INDIGENOUS FISHING AND FISHERS

Standing on a ferry chugging across Sydney Harbour, it's still possible to imagine the city as it was prior to colonisation – before the span of the bridge, before the marinas and yachts, before buildings were planted onto that sloping, rocky landscape. Pockets of bush still reach down towards the water, where gums and angophoras curl around sandstone coves carved out by the sea water.

Ferries stop at Mosman, Manly and Milsons Point, where fishers share the wharf with boats and commuters. They perch on folding chairs next to white buckets of bait, or they plonk down on the wooden beams, rod in hand, their legs dangling over the edge as they sit.

Yet these places were also occupied, named and fished, long before 'Sydney' appeared on any charts. And it's at one of these harbour places, at Kay-ye-my, or perhaps Goram Bullagong (present-day Manly Cove and Mosman Bay), that our first story of Indigenous fishing is set. (After all, Kiarabilli or Kiarabily – the site of present-day Milsons Point and Kirribilli – is believed to translate into English as 'good fishing spot'.)

Malgun – the amputation of the joint of a young girl's left little finger – is one of many Aboriginal fishing rites that was practised along much of the east coast of what's now known as Australia. Across the continent, diverse and adaptable fishing practices, recipes and rituals were a cornerstone of Indigenous life at the time of first contact – and many remain so to this day.

Like *keeparra* (the knocking out of teeth) and scarification, *malgun* is a custom rich with significance, an offering to the spirits. In this case, the little girl would be forever linked with the fish she had literally fed. And as these girls grew into women, that connection to the underwater world was held to offer good fortune and prowess with a fishing line.

It's thought that *malgun* was also about the practicalities of fishing, since a shorter left pinky could apparently wind a handline in more nimbly. The practice was observed among Aboriginal communities along the eastern seaboard of Australia. (And featured around the country in various forms.) But its meaning was frequently misunderstood in early colonial encounters and is still open for speculation.

To make the line, or *currejun/garradjun*, Gadigal fisherwomen used the bark or the tender fibres of young kurrajong trees, which they soaked and pounded or sometimes chewed, scraping off the outer layers with a shell. The pliable strands were then worked into fine strong thread. The women cast out their handlines and quickly drew them back in on the strike, hand over hand, before the fish could shake off the hook.

I like to picture the women sitting on a beach or around a fire as they made their string, humming, singing and chatting. They rolled the fibres along their thighs methodically, slowly turning them into lengths of delicate but durable fishing twine.

Even the name of this beautiful and distinctive tree provides a valuable historical link to a time when fishing dominated the physical, social and cultural life of coastal Aboriginal peoples. What they sang and nattered about, while swatting mosquitoes and shooing away curious children, we can only guess.

At the end of these lines, elegant fishhooks, or *burra*, made from carved abalone or turban shells were dropped over the side of their canoes, or *nowies*. Although in other parts of Australia, hooks made from a piece of tapered hardwood, bird talon or bone have also been found. These '*nowies* were nothing more than a large piece of bark tied up at both ends with vines', described the British officer Watkin Tench in his account of early Sydney.

Despite the *nowies*' apparent flimsiness, the fisherwomen were master skippers. They paddled across the bays and out through the Heads, waves slapping at the sides of their precarious little vessels. That mobility was essential for Aboriginal clans around the harbour – such as the Gadigal, Gayamaygal, Wangal and Darramurragal – who needed to chase shoals and find new grounds if the fishing was quiet at particular times of the year.

Small fires were lit in the *nowie* on a platform of clay and weed before the craft was launched into the water from a snug harbour cove. Then the fisherwoman perched inside and paddled to a favourite spot or two, often with a baby cradled in her lap and an infant on her shoulders or crouched beside her.

Out on the water, she chewed crustaceans and shellfish, spitting some out into the water before jigging her pearlescent hook up and down like a lure. This sort of berleying was practised all around Australia in the hope of generating a bit more action – thousands of years before punctured tins of cheap cat food dropped off the back of a tinnie to attract fish became the norm.

When a fisherwoman threw the line overboard, she waited for that strike and tug from a whiting, dory or snapper, which would be quickly hauled aboard and charred on the waiting fire. And she sang as she fished, her voice carrying across the bays and inlets and down through the water to the fish below.

Those fishing songs also captured the attention of colonists, like the colonial judge advocate David Collins, who described seeing Carangarang and Kurúbarabúla (the sister and wife of Bennelong, respectively) return from a canoe trip 'to procure fish' and they 'were keeping time with their paddles, responsive to the words of a song, in which they joined with much good humour and harmony'.

Some, like the French explorer Louis de Freycinet, were so transfixed by the songs they overheard bouncing over the water they attempted to write them down in musical notation.

While women were the anointed line fishers and shell-fish gatherers in many Aboriginal and Torres Strait Islander communities, spearfishing was largely the preserve of men – and this continues to be the case today. Hunters stalked the water's edge or stood in a canoe, looking for the telltale shadow of a dusky flathead or the flash of silver from a darting bream.

When the water was calm and clear enough, Aboriginal men around Warrane-Sydney Harbour and Kamay-Botany Bay were frequently seen lying across their *nowies*, faces fully submerged, peering through the cool blue with a spear at the ready. 'This they do with such certainty, as rarely to miss their aim,' wrote the painter and engraver John Heaviside Clark in 1813.

At night, Aboriginal fishermen took the canoes out onto the water with their flaming hand torches held aloft. The light lured the fish to the boat side where they were speared by a barbed prong whittled out of bone, shell or hardwood. In the muddy mangroves of northern Australia, fires were sometimes lit on creek banks to attract barramundi, which swam towards the light and suffered the same fate. Beautiful images from the early days of the colony depict country we can still see traces of today: folds in the landscape as it stretches out across the horizon, the bush reaching right down to the water's edge, protected sandy coves perfect for camping and fishing. They also show us the centrality of fishing to First Nations communities. These sources show how Aboriginal people fished and what they caught, like a juicy snapper flailing on the end of a spear, or a fisherwoman managing both an infant and a fishing line in her *nowie*. The skill of these fishers and the abundance of fish are lasting impressions from these visual records.

While early colonial sketches and paintings give wonderful snapshots of Aboriginal fishers, they do so from a European perspective. Written accounts are similarly revealing, and we can be grateful for the faithful record of fishing practices and winning catches they've produced. But we can't forget that these people viewed First Nations societies through a distinctly colonial lens.

The early colonial view of Australia was mostly curious and enlightened, and colonists were often captivated by the extraordinary skills of Aboriginal fishers, as well as their depth of knowledge about their Country. Yet they were also people of their time, who saw the British expansion in Australia as inevitable, and viewed Country with a lowercase 'c' – as a resource awaiting exploitation.

Sometimes, vital Indigenous perspectives creep in. Scars on the mighty trunks of river red gums, or canoe trees, along the banks and floodplains of the Murray River reveal an Aboriginal presence long before any European record. Enormous engravings of whales, fish and sharks etched into sandstone platforms around Sydney and into the rugged iron ore of Murujuga-Burrup Peninsula in Western Australia have a provenance hundreds and sometimes thousands of years older than any colonial etching or journal entry. Elaborate fish traps across the continent and the Torres Strait demonstrate intricate knowledge of seasonal and tidal fish aggregations.

Paintings in smoke-stained caves in northern Australia show equally distinctive Aboriginal readings of fishing feats and feasts. And the remnants of literally millions of Indigenous seafood meals can be seen in middens around the continent that cascade through dirt, sand and mud at the water's edge.

These 'Indigenous archives' give us a glimpse into fishing before European colonisation. They also reveal the ingenuity

INDIGENOUS ARCHAEOLOGY & MIDDENS

Indigenous material culture and cultural practices tell us important information about Indigenous fishing. Artworks and artefacts, along with language and oral histories, depict the kinds of fish Aboriginal communities caught, how they fished and what they ate.

Archaeological investigations also give valuable information about the ways Aboriginal people fished. For example, studies of women's skeletons from the Tasmanian and Victorian coasts show that many had a strange bone growth in their ear. The cause turned out to be closer to present-day lived experiences than we might think: these women had what's known as 'surfer's ear', a thickening of the bone to protect the inner ear from extreme cold temperatures. Such permanent physiological change, caused by the cold, turgid waters of the south-eastern coast, reveal just how often these fisherwomen inhabited the sea, swimming and diving for abalone.

Other excavation sites similarly confirm the centrality of fishing to Indigenous communities around the country. The term *midden* (an old Scandinavian word that literally means a dump for domestic waste) has taken on particular archaeological importance: the day-to-day ephemera and detritus of pre-contact Indigenous camps and communities tells us a lot about the food they ate, the tools they used and the materials they built, bartered and buried. Middens are like time capsules, stratified layers of rubbish that lay bare generations of eating habits and material culture. Analyses of fish bones and shellfish indicate the prevalence of certain species in particular areas over time; artefacts such as spearheads, fishhooks and tools show changing cultural practices and even trading patterns between groups. At times, these sites also point to mysterious absences, such as the lack of finfish in Tasmanian middens, which caused some scholars to controversially speculate that the whole island population might have simply stopped eating fish for 3000 years prior to European contact.

of pre-industrial First Nations communities, long before fish finders, weather apps and soft plastics.

Remnants of vast, curving fish traps, or *Ngunnhu*, made from river stones still lie near Brewarrina in central New South Wales. (There were even more *Ngunnhu* once, until they were pushed aside to make way for paddle-steamers taking the wool clip down to Adelaide in the late nineteenth century.)

In the early spring or during a large flow of fresh water after heavy rains, enormous numbers of fish would travel upriver, swelling the eddies and currents with a mass of writhing tails and fins. Aboriginal fishers – men and women from the Ngemba, Wonkamurra, Wailwan and Gomeroi nations – kept watch from grassy embankments above the river and, as soon as enough fish had entered the labyrinth of traps, they rolled large rocks across the openings, ensnaring them for a seasonal fish feast.

These traps and weirs were also an early form of fisheries management – well before government regulations and research organisations – and remnants can be seen right across central and western New South Wales. Juvenile fish were carried in curved wooden *coolamons* and released behind the barriers on the smaller tributaries as a way of boosting stocks and ensuring fish for seasons to come.

The Budj Bim eel traps at Lake Condah in south-west Victoria were designed, built and maintained by the Gunditjmara people, who operated the series of channels, locks and weirs. Built at least 6600 years ago, the traps have been redeveloped several times over several centuries, and they demonstrate an ecologically sustainable management of this freshwater eel fishery that was adapted and lasted for thousands of years. What's more, they can still be seen today.

Other traps were less permanent, but just as effective. When particular waterholes were low in the Baaka-Darling river system in New South Wales, Barkindji people living along the river used wooden stakes, logs and sometimes stones to build shallow pens that trapped fish, yabbies and eels for easy pickings.

The ill-fated explorer William John Wills described a similar 'arrangement for catching fish' somewhere north of Birdsville around the Georgina River, where he camped with Robert O'Hara Burke and the rest of their party in January 1861. The trap consisted of 'a small oval mud paddock about 12 feet by 8 feet, the sides of which were about nine inches above the bottom of the hole', he wrote. The 'top of the fence' was 'covered with long grass, so arranged that the ends of the blades overhung scantily by several inches the sides of the hole'.

Periods of drought and seasonal dry weather could change rivers from torrential, turgid flows to the most meagre trickle – a chain of muddy holes through the landscape. Across northern Australia, seasons of wet and dry charged the landscape with weather cycles that pushed water across the floodplains of the northern savannah in great sheets, and then inevitably dried them out again.

But even low water could mean good fishing, since the fish would be forced to aggregate in particular waterholes, where they could be readily trapped and caught. While the grass might be parched and brittle up on the banks, the water below was teeming with life; that was the time when Aboriginal people walked along the creek bottom, muddying the water and forcing the fish to rise and take in air where they were easily speared, clubbed or netted. In the Kimberley, when the dry season came and the floodwaters finally receded, rolls of spinifex were used to entangle fish that had been trapped in the remaining waterholes.

Artefacts such as spears, hooks and nets also help reconstruct some of the changing ways and means of Indigenous fishing that pre-date European colonisation and continue to be used and modified long after it. These relics are as beautiful as they were effective. Kangaroo tail tendon was used to bind fishhooks in northern Australia. The prongs of spears (fish gigs or fizgigs) were hardened and polished and then attached to the long shaft using pieces of thread daubed with resin.

Meanwhile, nets made from lengths of finely twisted twine were so carefully knotted together that when Governor Phillip showed them to the white women in the colony, the elegant loops reminded them of English lace. Those nets came in all shapes and sizes and were highly prized possessions. To strengthen the nets' fishing powers, Aboriginal people sang to them: their music and words, literally singing in the fish, were like charms for the Dreaming that cascaded through the weave.

In the area of what's now known as Sydney, coastal tribes used small hoop nets to pick up lobsters, which hid in the crevasses under rocky sandstone ledges on the edge of the harbour and along the beachside cliffs. Catch-and-cast nets trapped small numbers of fish in creeks and waterholes near the coast and could also be used to carry a feed of fish as families walked back to their camps through the well-worn walking tracks.

Further inland, Aboriginal people made large woven river nets, which would be held by hand or propped up along the bank. Once fixed in place, groups of people waded through the murky water, loudly beating the surface and driving the startled fish into the mesh. The nets were usually about 4 metres long and 1 metre deep – sizeable enough, considering every strand was gathered, spun and woven by hand. But one extraordinary account from the explorer Charles Sturt described how his exploration party on the Wambuul-Macquarie River in western New South Wales discovered a fishing net some 90 metres long in a Wiradjuri village they came across.

Other fishing methods have been recorded and described in oral histories, or they've been passed down and are practised still. These practices are a form of embodied or 'living archives', which is how we know about them today. Stories of women diving deep underwater for shellfish, walking out across the rocks at low tide pulling off abalone, or wading through billabongs to pick up turtles, are common in accounts from the time and are still maintained by many Indigenous communities around Australia and the Torres Strait Islands. Given such longstanding fishing connections, 'sea rights' have been increasingly recognised by governments in legislating fisheries management. Back on the beach or riverbank, a fire is inevitably on the go in anticipation of a fresh catch. The fish is usually chucked on whole, then eaten, guts and all.

The Catch

Some of the environmental knowledge used by Traditional Owners seems astonishing in today's context of mass-produced fishing lures and frozen bait from the local servo. One account from northern Australia described a particularly large Golden Orb spider carefully killed to preserve its abdomen, which was then gently squeezed to milk its adhesive goo. Small fish, attracted to the carcass, would then get stuck to the dead spider before being delicately lifted ashore by nimble hands. Fish poisoning, using various berries, roots, leaves and stems, was also common throughout Australia. In the Kimberley around the Goonoonoorrang-Ord River in Western Australia, Traditional Owners such as the Miriuwung, Kuluwaring and Gajerrabeng used crushed leaves from the freshwater mangrove (*malawarn*) to poison their prey, sweeping branches through the water until stunned fish started floating belly up.

Along the east coast it was wattle leaves that did the damage. The sunny, fragrant puffballs of two common acacias (*Acacia implexa* and *Acacia longifolia*) belie their potency as a fish poison. Once absorbed through the gills, antigens from the bruised leaves were quickly catastrophic for fish in little waterholes and billabongs. There are even accounts of eels gliding out of the water and into the bush along the Clarence River in northern New South Wales (known as *Boorimbah* to the Bundjalung and *Ngunitiji* to the Yaygir) in an attempt to escape poisoning from Aboriginal fishers.

Although these poisoning methods apparently had no effect on the edibility of the fish, the trick was to carefully manage the immersion of these toxic branches in the water – giving just enough poison to stun the fish, but not enough to knock out the whole waterhole.

That intimate knowledge and understanding of Country and its seasons wasn't readily apparent to the early colonists. Watkin Tench was so perplexed by the unpredictability of fishing in Australia that he complained about spending all night out on Sydney Harbour for little result. The 'universal voice of all professed fishermen', he lamented in the 1790s in *A Complete Account of the Settlement at Port Jackson*, was that they had 'never fished in a country where success was so precarious and uncertain'.

It was knowledge that came slowly to the colonists, over several generations. William Scott, the New South Wales colonial astronomer from 1856 to 1862, observed how the Worimi people were able to anticipate fishing seasons around Port Stephens on the New South Wales Mid North Coast. 'By some unerring instinct the blacks knew within a day when the first of the great shoals [of sea mullet] would appear through the heads,' he explained.

For the Yolŋu in Arnhem Land, flowering of stringybark trees coincides with the shrinking of waterholes, where fish can be more readily netted and speared, or poisoned. And when the Dharawal people of the Kamay and Shoalhaven region in New South Wales see the golden wattle flowers of the *Kai'arrewan* (*Acacia binervia*), they know that the fish will be running in the rivers and prawns will be schooling in estuarine shallows.

In Queensland the movement and population of particular fish species have their own corresponding sign on land. The extent of the annual sea-mullet run in the cool winter months can be predicted by the numbers of rainbow lorikeets in late autumn; if magpies are scarce in winter, numbers of luderick will also be low; and when the bush is ablaze with the fragrant sunny blooms of coastal wattle in early spring, surging schools of tailor can be expected just offshore. Perhaps climate change may shift these fishing markers in the natural world?

This knowledge was acquired by Australia's Indigenous peoples through generations of observation and practice. What's more, that deep understanding was as much about the spirit world as the natural. Neither can be properly comprehended without reference to the other – although our own contemporary insights are often sketchy, since the sporadic observations of colonists are frequently the only available historical sources we have of Indigenous fishing practices.

Practical understanding was intimately entwined with spiritual readings of the land. First Nations Dreamings are systems of cultural values and observations: they created the world and are reflected in day-to-day observations of that life. These 'spiritscapes', as the archaeologist Ian McNiven has called them, infused Country with cosmology. The natural and spirit worlds were one and the same. Country wasn't inanimate – it could feel and do. And for many Indigenous people to this day, that knowledge remains a shaping, dynamic belief system.

There are accounts on the South Australian coastline of Aboriginal people ritually singing in dolphins or sharks to herd fish into constructed or natural enclosures on the Eyre and Yorke peninsulas. In Twofold Bay, on Yuin Country in southern New

South Wales, dolphins were similarly used to herd fish, and a totemic bond between killer whales and Aboriginal people was also observed and documented.

Why did Aboriginal communities around Sydney avoid eating sharks and stingrays? No one really knows the source of this taboo. The water was full of them, but they were only ever eaten during times of food scarcity. William Bradley, a first lieutenant on the First Fleet, observed Aboriginal people catching 'jew fish, snapper, mullet, mackerel, whiting, dory, rock cod and leather-jacket' throughout the summer, but they didn't keep the sharks or rays. 'There are great numbers of the sting ray and shark, both of which I have seen the natives throw away when given to them and often refuse them when offered,' he noted.

In Lutruwita-Tasmania, archaeological excavations of middens suggest Palawa people mysteriously avoided eating finfish altogether for the 3000 years prior to colonisation, hunting mammals and scavenging shellfish instead. Was it spiritual? A response to some sort of poisoning event? Or an economic decision to harvest easier resources (such as seals and abalone)? Did the community lose their knowledge of fishing, as some have argued? Or did they perhaps dispose of the bones somewhere else? No one really knows.

Some forms of Indigenous fishing inevitably became lost as Traditional Owners were dispossessed and disenfranchised of their lands and fisheries following the expansion of the colonial frontier post-1788. Many Indigenous practices were eventually superseded by new technologies. Other Indigenous fishers became active in the establishment of the commercial fishing industry in Australia, maintaining strong links to traditional knowledges, as well as adapting to modern fishing approaches and technologies.

Indigenous peoples have played and continue to play a prominent role in the history of Australian fishing. Despite the ruptures of colonisation, the cultural and social cleavages wrought by disease, as well as frontier violence and dispossession, they remain a visible and vital part of Australian fishing culture as commercial and recreational fishers, industry partners and Traditional Owners of the vast natural resource that is Australia's fisheries.

On 28 April 1770, a British naval research vessel pushes through the breakers on the edge of Botany Bay. This is the first time European eyes have peered across Kamay's blue waters. 'The land this morn appeard Cliffy and barren without wood,' wrote Joseph Banks, the expedition's botanist. 'An opening appearing like a harbour was seen, and we stood directly in for it.' Once inside, they're protected from the chop rolling in off the Tasman and find themselves surrounded by mangroves and thick sandy scrub. It's the middle of autumn, just before the ocean temperatures around Sydney dip for winter, and the fish are still plentiful.

CHAPTER 2

'PROCURABLE IN THE UTMOST ABUNDANCE' COLONIAL ENCOUNTERS

On that voyage of discovery, Captain James Cook had already witnessed the transit of Venus in Tahiti, before circumnavigating and mapping the islands of Aotearoa New Zealand. After that famous visit to Kamay-Botany Bay, he'd go on to annex the entire eastern coast of what we now know as Australia, on behalf of King George III.

As the HMS *Endeavour* sailed in past the heads of the bay, Joseph Banks saw several fishing parties, including 'four small canoes; in each of these was one man who held in his hand a long pole with which he struck fish'. And when the sun went down on their first night in Australia, Banks peered out over the ship's deck and saw 'many moving lights' bobbing along the water through the darkness. He understood them to be night fishers – Gwaegal or Gameygal people using firesticks to attract fish like snapper and bream to the side of their *nowies*. They were easy pickings for the skilled spearfishermen, who tossed them onto the fire beds sitting at the ends of their canoes.

In that wide, shallow bay, surrounded by coastal shrub and sand dunes, the *Endeavour* dropped anchor and the crew busied themselves on land, collecting botanical specimens, looking for fresh water, initiating halting, cautious, occasionally confrontational meetings with Dharawal people and trying their luck with the local fish.

They didn't have to wait long. On 30 April 1770, two days after their arrival, Cook described returning from an exploratory sortie to find some of his crew fishing in a cove on the northern side of the bay – near present-day Yarra Bay or, perhaps, Congwong Bay. The men used a seine, a type of net that's dragged through the water like an open purse, and the ends are slowly brought together to trap the fish. They 'caught about 300 pounds weight of fish', wrote Cook in his journal, after only '3 or 4 hauls' of the net.

I snorkel around this area often: luderick school over the rounded rocky platforms picking at sea lettuce, while wrasse and morwong hide in the small crevasses below, and whiting dart across the sandy bottom. But the thought of seeing 140 kilograms of fish there, let alone netting them in a few speculative short hauls, seems incomprehensible today.

In 1770, the fishing was by all accounts plentiful. On 4 May, Banks similarly recorded a seine 'hawld . . . upon a sandy beach' filled with a 'great plenty of small fish'. And, when they got back to the *Endeavour*, they found the second lieutenant,

John Gore, with a catch of enormous rays he'd speared. There was evidently no colonial taboo on eating these graceful giants.

The largest of the catch was 239 pounds – about 108 kilograms – 'when his gutts were taken out'. These were almost certainly smooth rays, a large and placid species that frequents boat ramps and filleting tables in the hope of scoring an easy meal. Patrolling the sandy shallows of a Kamay high tide, and largely left alone by local Aboriginal people, they would have been relatively easy pickings for the visitors.

Banks spent the following day roaming the coastal bush collecting specimens to take back to England, while Gore again busied himself spearfishing and managed to grab more stingrays. These were even bigger – the largest weighed in at a hefty 336 pounds (152 kilograms), 'without his gutts', Banks again noted.

The next day, they departed, feasting on their giant catch as they sailed up the coast. After confidently planting the Union Jack on Possession Island in the Torres Strait, they continued to head north and then west, passing through the Arafura Sea and on to South-East Asia. There they would have crossed over the sea routes of the Macassan trepang fishers. The Macassans were regular visitors to the coastal waters of Arnhem Land, in the Northern Territory, and the Kimberley, in Western Australia, where they fished for sea cucumber and traded with local Aboriginal people.

But, on that May evening, it was the Botany Bay rays that caught Banks' attention: 'Went to sea this morn with a fair breeze of wind,' he penned in his journal, and 'dind to day upon the stingray and his tripe'. The flesh wasn't quite to everybody's liking, Banks admitted, but 'the tripe every body thought excellent', particularly since it was served with a dish of warrigal greens foraged from the shores of the bay.

Given that apparently boundless bounty of land and resources, it's not surprising that Cook's map of Australia didn't gather dust in a bottom drawer back in England. Seventeen years after his exploratory journey, Australia was again the destination for a monumental British expedition.

In May 1787, four months after Britain decided to tackle its overflowing jails by sending the problem as far away as possible, eleven ships set off across the seas headed for Kamay-Botany Bay. Their holds were filled with about 800 convicts and supplies, 300 gallons of brandy, 18 turkeys, 700 gimlets and 327 pairs of women's stockings (among other essential items). Also stored away in the bowels of those creaking sailboats were 14 fishing nets, 8000 fishhooks and 576 lines.

It's a fascinating window into a colonial mentality – the idea that you can simply 'set up shop' on the other side of the world. And to that end the list shows not simply the *stuff* colonists thought they needed – like gimlets and stockings – but some of their cultural and social practices, too, such as sewing, leatherwork, carpentry, whaling, agriculture, masonry, milling, religion, blacksmithing, and, of course, fishing.

No one on that voyage had ever been to Australia before. The closest Captain Arthur Phillip (who later became the first governor of New South Wales) had come to Botany Bay was reading accounts from Cook's earlier expedition across

MACASSANS

The Macassans were Muslim fishermen from Java who plied the waters along the northern coast of Australia searching for trepang several hundred years before European colonisation. Trepang is a type of sea cucumber, or bêche-de-mer, a rather unfortunate-looking echinoderm that slithers very slowly around the tropical ocean rock pools of northern Australia.

Speared at low tide, boiled and then smoked, the preserved trepang were apparently irresistible to Chinese traders. It was prized for its jelly-like texture, its flavour-enhancing qualities and its power as a stimulant and aphrodisiac – hence the burgeoning trade nearly 500 years ago.

The Macassans came to Australia in small boats, their sails filled by the winds of the north-west monsoon. They negotiated fishing rights with First Nations peoples right across the north, harvested and preserved the trepang, and then returned to Java on the south-east winds some months later when the seasons changed.

By the nineteenth century, perhaps a thousand or so Macassans were visiting northern Australia every year to fish for trepang. They fished the warm waters between the Kimberley and Cape York and exchanged items, such as cloth, tobacco, metal axes and knives, rice and gin, with local Aboriginal communities, who traded items such as turtle-shell, pearls and even employment in return.

Evidence of their fishing is still visible today: in the archaeological remains that include pieces of metal, broken pottery and glass, coins, fishhooks and broken clay pipes from the remains of trepang-processing plants at Port Essington, Anuru Bay and Groote Eylandt in the Northern Territory; in the stands of the tamarind trees introduced by the Macassans that can still be seen along the Arnhem and Kimberley coasts; and the remnants of Macassar vocabulary and religion in Yolŋu language and Dreaming stories.

the Pacific. Phillip knew there'd be fish because of those colossal hauls from Botany Bay that the crew on Cook's ship had described.

Given such successes, it's no surprise that tucked away in the holds of the First Fleet were boxes of tackle procured for the colony and its apparent fishing largesse. Within a few days of arriving, in January 1788, it had already been put to use.

Mirroring the experiences of Cook's crew, the First Fleeters quickly found the fishing in Australia worth writing home about. Second Lieutenant Ralph Clark and surgeon George Worgan described in their published journals catches of a 'great manny of fish' and of a 'very successful haul of Fish in the Seine' while the fleet was anchored in Kamay-Botany Bay.

On 23 January, as Phillip was scouting out the suitability of Port Jackson for the future settlement, seaman Jacob Nagle couldn't resist throwing a line in while he waited for Governor Phillip's return. 'I being the boat keeper, I had to remain in the boat,' he explained in his journal. 'I hove my line over' and 'hal'd up a large black brim'. When Phillip returned to the boat he turned to Nagle and saw the sizeable bream. '"Recollect," said he, "that you are the first white man that ever caught a fish in Sidney Cove where the town is to be built."'

Towards the end of the following spring, one haul of fish was so large, wrote David Collins, the colony's newly minted judge advocate, that it actually broke the net. It 'burst at the moment of landing', he described with dramatic flourish. Loads spilled back into the water and the fishers were left pondering just how much they'd lost. Collins speculated that if the haul had been landed, the entire catch could 'have served the settlement [of over 1000 people] for a day'. Tales of fishing bounties often featured in early colonial accounts, and they were obviously memorable enough to note down at the time – who wouldn't brag that the nets had broken with an enormous haul, or that they'd caught forty-seven large snapper on a single outing? Fishing in Sydney Harbour today, such tales seem almost unbelievable.

First impressions weren't always so effusive, however. Collins described any reliance on fishing in the colony as 'precarious'. And, in April 1788, Governor Phillip offered this perplexed assessment of Australian fishing: 'Fish affords, in this place, only an uncertain resource,' he mused. On 'some days great quantities are caught . . . but at times it is very scarce'.

In fact, within months, the fishing had gone quiet and the colony faced imminent starvation. Things were so desperate that Governor Phillip directed a convict rope maker to draw on the knowledge of Aboriginal women from the harbour tribes and spin fishing lines from the bark of the kurrajong tree as they did, in the hopes that these would help the colony boost its dwindling stores. It was tacit recognition of Aboriginal peoples' deep knowledge and skill.

The colonists were baffled by the unpredictability of the fishing. Was the water too cold? Did the fish go somewhere else in winter? It seemed the continent's apparent abundance was also alarmingly temperamental.

That bemusing paradox of Australia's natural resources continued inland, as successive waves of explorers headed out across the continent. Motivated by the pursuit of scientific knowledge and imperial fame, these ventures into the continent's interior were at once voyages of discovery and colonial acquisition.

Their routes, like tiny ribbons of Morse code snaking around the country, would be immortalised in the maps of school textbooks for generations to come. And their journeys were Homeric. Some described how this harsh, remote country yielded astonishing harvests; others, meanwhile, perished from starvation surrounded by plenty.

In 1817, Governor Lachlan Macquarie appointed John Oxley to survey the Lachlan River in central New South Wales 'to ascertain the real course . . . of the Lachlan . . . and whether it falls into the sea, or into some inland lake'. Like colonial fishers on the coast, Oxley was struck by the enigmatic unpredictability of Australia's natural world.

The land seemed barren and unsuited for pastoralism, he observed, yet the river teemed with life. 'If however the country itself is poor, the river is rich in the most excellent fish, procurable in the utmost abundance,' Oxley penned in his journal. 'One man in less than an hour caught eighteen large fish, one of which was a curiosity from its immense size, and the beauty of its colours.' The fish he referred to, probably a generous-sized Murray cod, 'weighed entire 70 pounds'. And that wasn't the only one, Oxley added: 'Most of the other fish taken this evening weighed from 15 to 30 pounds each.'

This wasn't simply a lucky afternoon casting a line from the riverbank. Littered through the journal entries of these explorers are descriptions of the numerous fish they saw, heard and pulled out of Australian rivers, estuaries and billabongs, as well as of the extensive Indigenous fishing parties, fish traps and technologies they encountered. Fish filled the waterways – from the seasonal rivers of the tropical north to the most arid interior.

On his 5000-kilometre trek from Moreton Bay to Port Essington, the naturalist and explorer Ludwig Leichhardt described being kept awake by a vigorous and mysterious splashing – probably barramundi – as he camped by Comet Creek, near Emerald, in central Queensland. It was January 1845, the height of summer, and traversing the scrubby, rocky country had taken its toll on the entire party, including Leichhardt's horses and cattle. But as they lay down to rest, the water came to life. Leichhardt wrote that it was 'teeming with fish, apparently of considerable size, as their splashing startled me several times during the night, and made me believe, for the moment, that a large tribe of natives were bathing'.

Even William John Wills, who famously walked from Melbourne to the Gulf of Carpentaria with Robert O'Hara Burke in the 1860s, had been surprised by the number of fish in central Australia, and the fishing successes and knowledges of the Aboriginal people who caught them.

On their way north, Wills described complex fish traps as well as 'presents of fish' given to the exploration party, 'for which we gave them some beads and matches'. The fish were 'a most valuable addition to our rations', wrote Wills, a diligent and lucid diarist. 'They were of the same kind as we had found elsewhere, but finer, being from nine to ten inches long, and two to three inches deep, and in such good condition that they might have been fried in their own fat.'

Yet, after months of deprivation and an agonising bungle in which their reconnaissance party was missed, Burke and Wills perished on the banks of Cooper Creek in central Australia. They were surrounded by a thriving Yandruwandha Aboriginal community and a river full of fish.

When explorers had no luck finding fish, it was often because Aboriginal fishers got in first. In his book *Three Expeditions into the Interior of Eastern Australia*, the surveyor Thomas Mitchell described Aboriginal groups (probably Ngemba or Wiradjuri people) mocking and chuckling from the riverbank when his party unknowingly dropped their lines into spots that had been recently harvested. To fish these waterholes, Aboriginal women pushed sieve-like traps, made of 'long, twisted dry grass', along their length to cordon off the fish. If Mitchell's men 'began to fish' at places along the Bogan River 'where a tribe had recently been', he wrote, Aboriginal people nearby would 'laugh most heartily at the hopeless attempt'.

It was a nod to the drama fishing produces in the most unexpected places; it also revealed the vast knowledge imbalance between Traditional Owners and the colonial interlopers. Words like 'discover' and 'pioneer', which are associated with Australia's exploration history, seem pitifully inadequate when the whole continent and coastline had been mapped long before colonial paper versions were produced. Compared with thousands of years of inherited understanding and observation, a colonial traipse across Country was a mere blip.

Yet, with each journey of exploration across sea and land, with every line and net dropped into the water, colonists' knowledge of Australia's fish and how to catch them grew. Partly that knowledge was covetous – fish were seen as a resource to be exploited and capitalised upon. But the colonial project wasn't simply a quest for global power and control of the world's resources; it also satisfied a thirst for knowledge and scientific prowess. Knowledge, in and of itself, was a form of colonial power.

This was a high point of the European Enlightenment, that broad movement of reason and rationality which contended that the world could be understood and improved with scientific and philosophical deduction. As well as impelling ever-increasing concentric waves of global exploration and 'discovery', the eighteenth and nineteenth centuries saw the consolidation of fields of knowledge such as natural history and earth sciences. Carl Linnaeus's taxonomy of the natural world in 1735 and the publication of Charles Darwin's *On the Origin of Species* in 1859 are two important examples from this period that continue to influence our understanding of the natural sciences.

In an age of discovery and exploration, fish also became a site of colonial advancement and authority in Australia. The nineteenth century was an era of great scientific expansion, after all, which saw a proliferation of public collections in museums and exhibitions, the professionalisation of scientific disciplines and the classification of the natural world.

In line with this growing scientific influence and reach, Governor Ralph Darling had established a colonial museum in Sydney by 1827 and, along with it, created the position of Colonial Zoologist, a role tasked with identifying and monitoring different animal species, including fish. The science of Australian ichthyology, of understanding Australia's fish species and how they fitted into the wider natural world, was also gaining interest among scientists internationally, including Darwin. With over 4000 different species, there was no shortage of information to uncover and knowledge to acquire.

The question was: what would they do with all these fish?

263 MENDING THE NETS. PHOTO BY JUDGES

The boat glides out of Albany and sails across the sheltered waters of Princess Royal Harbour. A breeze skims across the bay and fills the sails — just enough to push the little craft along into the incoming tide to set the nets. There's plenty to catch here, and the fisherman fills his woven baskets with herring, whiting and bream, with a few skipjack and pike thrown in for good measure. But there's not much point chasing the big hauls, since the fish go putrid after a day or two ashore — and anything left over has to be buried.

CHAPTER 3

'CEASELESS AND OFTEN WANTON PROCESS OF NETTING' EARLY INDUSTRY

Sources from the early days of colonial fishing are patchy, with not much more than the occasional newspaper report and a series of inquiries into the management of fisheries, along with folklore handed down the generations by fishing communities.

Once pieced together, however, they reveal a sense of the overwhelming, albeit inconsistent, bounty of Australia's natural world in the mid to late nineteenth century. They also show a prevailing attitude among colonial society about the obligation to exploit apparently untapped natural resources.

Despite the unpredictability of this bounty, Australia's early commercial fishers described what we can only read today as some sort of fishing Eden: the sea floor off the west coast of Tasmania carpeted red with crayfish; fish so thick that nets could be set at any time of the day; an 'astonishing magnitude' of Australian salmon; and mountains of mullet that migrated annually up the continent's east coast.

Although some fish, like the humble wirrah, were notable for being decidedly uninspiring, with 'the flavour and consistency of leather', as scientist (and Catholic priest) Julian Edmund Tenison-Woods lamented in *Fish and Fisheries of New South Wales* in 1883, 'which no sauce or cooking can change'. (Not much has changed there, historically – my grandmother referred to wirrah as 'old boot' if one was ever brought into her kitchen.)

Apart from the odd culinary disappointment, tales of Australian fishing meccas echoed early colonial encounters in other parts of the New World, where Atlantic sturgeon up to 18 feet long (5.5 metres) and weighing 800 kilograms were recorded in Chesapeake Bay, on the Virginia coast. Staggering Chinook salmon runs swelled the Columbia and Vancouver rivers on the west coast of North America, and gigantic schools of cod filled the icy waters off the north-east of the continent.

If anything, the main challenge faced by the early Australian fishing industry was how to process the number of fish they were catching. The warm climate and the absence of ice manufacturing until the 1850s and 1860s meant that preserving fish for market was much more difficult than in the fisheries they had left behind in Britain and Europe. A sultry Sydney December afternoon or a gritty, dusty north wind descending on the cities of Adelaide and Melbourne hardly compared to the conditions for fisheries on the North Sea.

One report on the New South Wales fisheries from 1871 gives voice to that sense of disappointment and lost opportunity: 'in summer considerably more fish are thrown away from stress of weather, and the effect upon fish of a hot, muggy night in a slimy boat, than are consumed by the entire metropolis'.

Even with the arrival of ice, most fishers in their wooden ketches and cutters were far from the ice factories of Sydney and Melbourne. And it was simply impossible until the turn of the twentieth century to reliably transport fresh fish beyond the small fishing communities that procured them.

Until central fish markets were built late in the nineteenth century, the fish – if they made it to town – were sold door to door by hawkers who walked the streets early to avoid the heat of the day and weren't able to cart great quantities around by hand. Unless you fished yourself, eating seafood wasn't a day-to-day proposition for most people in the larger Australian cities in the nineteenth century.

A report by the commission into New South Wales fisheries in 1880 explained how there were several places even in Sydney where fish were rarely if ever seen on local dining tables. And, where people had become unaccustomed to eating fish, they seldom if ever thought of purchasing it. It wasn't uncommon to find badly decomposed fish on display in retail shops with the bones sticking out from the rotting flesh.

For some, the risk of spoilage through transportation was too great. Rather than face the prospect of getting nothing from buyers in town upon the arrival of yet another load of stinking snapper or mullet, fishing families often traded their catch within their own small communities, bartering fish for vegetables, beef, mutton, chickens and eggs.

Small amounts of fish were preserved in shanty smoke-houses, slapped together out of paperbark and tea tree. The rest went to farmers as fertiliser. Tasmanian fisher Bill Richards remembered farmers coming 'down with a horse and cart' until the 1920s to fetch barracouta for their plants. 'When the 'couta were very plentiful and the boats were catching more than could be handled at the smoking sheds, they'd run them down the channel to the farmers who bought them for manure,' he described. 'They used to put them around apple trees and rasp-berry canes – four 'couta to an apple tree, half a 'couta to a raspberry cane.'

Others sold their surplus to Chinese fish curers, commu-nities of which had popped up all around the Australian coast and further inland, from the south of the continent up to Darwin, following the Victorian gold rushes in the 1850s. Salted, sun-dried fish were packed in hessian bags and pickled fish were stored in timber casks ready for transportation to Chinese communities of miners, market gardeners and busi-nesspeople, for whom the fish was a welcome source of protein and traditional fare.

These preserved fish were reviled by the broader colonial community in Australia, who repeatedly described them as 'revolting' and 'detestable'. But without any reliable means of transporting their catch, commercial fishers were reliant on the fish curers for their livelihood.

The scale of this early demand for cured fish also demonstrates the size of the Chinese community in Australia in the second half of the nineteenth century. Lake Macquarie alone once supported 200 Chinese fish curers. But, by the early 1900s, pushed by increasingly xenophobic sentiment and the White Australia policy, and pulled by new leads for gold in places like New Zealand, much of the Chinese population had left Australia. Many returned to China and the demand for cured fish declined dramatically.

It's difficult to judge this relationship through a contemporary lens. There were high levels of racism around the country in the nineteenth century and the colonial population clearly felt the fish manufactured by the Chinese curers was unpalatable. In 1910, the South Australian *Fisheries Act* was even amended so that fishing licences, which had begun to be introduced in various colonies from the late nineteenth century, could only be held by natural-born or naturalised British subjects. It was a move explicitly designed to exclude Chinese people from Australia's fisheries.

Yet those same British subjects were reliant on that intercultural interaction for their economic survival. In fact, given the lack of infrastructure to keep fish fresh, the whole fishing industry depended on it.

Did they do business through gritted teeth or with welcome commerce? There was probably a bit of both. Given what we know about the prevalence of xenophobia and the political campaigns for a 'white' Australia in the nineteenth century, this cross-cultural co-dependence between the fishers and their

Chinese market shows the complexity and contradiction of lives in the past that historical research can uncover.

While early fishers were limited by the problems of preservation (not including Chinese curing), industries like sealing and whaling thrived, providing the bulk of Australian industry and exports well into the nineteenth century. While not strictly fisheries, their dominance of the colonial export economy highlights the technological limitations of fishing before the twentieth century – baleen, oil and pelts don't perish like fish.

Fisheries that relied less on refrigeration were also much more robust. Pearl fishers scoured the tropical waters off the north Queensland and Kimberley coasts. Others dived for trochus shells, hauling great mountains of shellfish onto elegant long luggers that seasonally scoured the northern coasts looking for the valuable shellfish, which were used for jewellery, ornaments and fashion. Compare that catch to the Lake Macquarie mullet that were transported by horse and cart to Newcastle and then by boat to Sydney – all without refrigeration.

Crayfish could also be kept alive for several days after capture, while oysters could survive up to two weeks in their shells before turning bad and were a major source of seafood consumption. Oyster bars and saloons popped up in centres like Brisbane, Sydney, Perth and Melbourne throughout the second half of the nineteenth century. The oysters were fresh, tasty and apparently abundant.

But there were also problems with the industry. Early methods of commercial oyster fishing were particularly

WHALING

Whaling was the first export industry in colonial Australia, and the colony's first large-scale commercial 'fishery', as it was known in those days. Whales were a valuable resource. Suffocating whale-bone corsets were all the rage in women's fashion during the eighteenth and nineteenth centuries, while the oil rendered from their generous blubber was in high demand following the insatiable march of industrialisation.

Heavy machinery needed constant lubrication and grease, and the manufacturing industries required lighting to work through the night. In homes and businesses across Europe and the colonies, whale-oil lanterns belched out acrid black smoke while people tried to read the news or write correspondence by the meagre lantern glow after dark.

By the early nineteenth century, whaling was the largest industry in Australia. Hundreds of whaling boats from all over the world sailed up and down the eastern seaboard of the continent, hunting whales to bring into one of the whaling stations dotted along the coast. Using harpoons thrown from small boats, the whalers secured their catch in coastal bays and inlets, dragging the carcasses to nearby whaling stations to be processed. It was dangerous and backbreaking work. By 1828, there were twenty-one whalers based out of Sydney Harbour alone – and the noise and stench from the boiling blubber forced the operations to move to more remote coves on the north shore, away from the growing township.

This sort of bay-based whaling lasted until petroleum eventually superseded whale oil in the mid-nineteenth century and the gold rushes lured swathes of itinerant whalers from their boats. A big resurgence of whaling then occurred at around the turn of the twentieth century, following the development of the harpoon gun and steam-powered factory ships that made profitable catches further offshore suddenly possible. Like other Australian fisheries, however, this large-scale mechanisation had immediate and catastrophic effects on stock numbers, and the number of whales in Australian waters plummeted accordingly. By 1962, there were estimates of only 200 to 500 humpback whales left and, in 1978, commercial whaling ceased in Australia. It's thought that the pre-whaling population of humpback whales was around 75,000 to 100,000.

Since commercial whaling ended, stocks have rebounded. The whalers have been replaced with whale watchers, and the rusting processing plants in Eden, Albany and elsewhere are firmly on the heritage trail for historical tourism.

destructive. Whole bays were dredged with the bars and iron mesh bags that hung off the stern of their boats. These contraptions were like underwater ploughs dragged along the seabed, picking up everything in their path.

Oysters, sea grasses, shells, slugs, crabs and small fish were unsparingly vacuumed into the dredges. Despite the picturesque scene the oyster fishers made in their little sailboats as they gently glided across the water, underneath it was rather more brutal.

Whole bays were quickly denuded of oysters in this fashion. The industry came under even more pressure because the lime extracted from incinerated oyster shells was an essential component in the early building industry in Australia. As stocks diminished with the dredging of ever more seabeds, there was considerable tension between the food and construction industries, and eventually the burning of live oysters was banned in Queensland in 1863 and then in New South Wales in 1868.

Until the advent of oyster farming, one of the earliest forms of aquaculture, oyster fishers had to constantly search for new grounds to dredge. This wasn't initially seen as a problem because oysters were apparently limitless, as this correspondent for the *Sydney Mail and New South Wales Advertiser* in 1871 explained: 'Sydney . . . need not be at all alarmed for the supply of oysters in her market, for no sooner is the wealth of one river exhausted than the dredgers can turn to another.'

But the system was unsustainable and, by the 1890s, the oyster industry was in serious decline. The fisheries scientist William Saville-Kent wrote a two-part article for the *Brisbane*

Courier in 1891 cataloguing a legacy of the oyster's demise, and a deep concern for the future of fisheries right around the country. 'Insatiable greed and over dredging,' he lamented, had 'reduced these prolific natural beds to the very verge of extinction'.

Oyster fishing was so indiscriminate that some of the earliest fisheries legislation in Victoria (as well as in Queensland, South Australia, New South Wales and Tasmania) concerned the management of oysters. And by the 1880s there had been several attempts made to reseed and restock depleted oyster beds, with mixed results.

Oyster fisheries were the victim of their own versatility. They were relatively non-perishable and were essential in the early building industry. Until their depletion, they were also abundant.

For the fin fishers, the next best thing to refrigeration was keeping the fish alive for as long as possible. Around Kangaroo Island in South Australia, for example, fishers handlining for whiting kept the fish in boat wells (storage tanks built into the boat) before sailing back to Adelaide. Others preferred the practice of 'mortgaging' – constructing large pens in estuaries and bays to keep any surplus fish in the water until they could be transported and sold.

Images and oral histories from this period reveal the perilous work of these early commercial fishers, who daily battled the elements looking for a catch without the benefits of engines or EPIRBs (emergency position indicating radio beacons). Fishing grounds were memorised by sighting landmarks. At night, they navigated by the stars, rowing or sailing out to the fishing grounds to set their nets, pots or longlines. Bad weather meant risking lives in handmade wooden boats, without a GPS (global positioning system) or radio, or it meant camping out with only a sail for shelter. It was a meagre, dangerous existence.

It's hard to imagine how these early commercial fishers would see our safety regulations today. Would they scoff at our mandatory life jackets and two-way radios? Would they think we were soft for jetting out across bars with huge outboards, rather than sailing or rowing out with the tide? Or would they look at all that gear with eager eyes and think, 'If only I'd had that'?

Commercial fishing back then was also grindingly hard work, most of it done by hand. Fishing nets made from cotton or hemp rotted easily and had to be tanned weekly or fortnightly. Ironbark or black-wattle fibres were boiled in great vats with the nets, so the tannins that leached from the bark temporarily protected the nets from sea water and jellyfish acid; nets were repaired by hand in backyards or by docks; crayfish pots were woven together using pliable canes, from tea-trees, for example, gathered from the bush.

New technology was risky and expensive. Even with the advent of engines in the early twentieth century, most small-scale family fishing operations couldn't even afford the fuel outlay, let alone engine costs. By the 1920s, crayfishers in Tasmania still rowed out to collect their pots every day – there were no outboards and the little boats had no freezers to store bait. Their lives are only a generation or two removed from our own, but the work lives they led seem almost unrecognisable by today's norms.

Inland, small dinghies and paddle-steamers plodded up and down the endlessly shifting waterways, setting baited drum nets, crosslines and sometimes gillnets between the snags and sandbars. Vast numbers of freshwater fish, particularly Murray cod, sustained a large, commercial fishery based mainly on the Murray and Murrumbidgee rivers. The cod were so big these fishers were known colloquially as 'Murray whalers'. And, by 1883, the Murray River fishery formed a considerable part of the fish supply to Melbourne, as well as to other cities and towns in Victoria and South Australia.

While the fishing industry was pretty rudimentary until the mid-twentieth century, its impact was far from it – both on the fisheries it touched and the Indigenous peoples who had managed them before colonisation. In the early days of the colony, contest over the ownership and control of fisheries was not uncommon, and sometimes became violent.

Only weeks after arriving in Port Jackson, two convict rush-cutters were murdered, likely on Wangal land, in retaliation for stealing a fishing *nowie*: 'They had been seen with a canoe,' Governor Phillip described, 'which they had taken from one of the fishing places.' Convicts who were caught stealing fishing tackle faced severe punishment.

Over time, the interactions between settler-colonists and Aboriginal peoples became more established but no less fraught. Sealers inhabited shacks on remote rocky islands off the southern coastlines of mainland Australia and Tasmania, and frequently forced Aboriginal women to cohabit with them in their precarious, cold and windy settlements. There are accounts of Aboriginal pearl divers made to work for nothing, diving 'naked' – meaning they dived without a snorkel, mask or oxygen – in the deep waters off Shark Bay in Western Australia. In northern Queensland and the Torres Strait, Aboriginal people and Torres Strait Islanders worked for a pittance, or nothing, on the pearling and trochus fleets, along with South Sea Islanders who'd been abducted from their homes and made to dive. It was dangerous work across the industry: sharks, the bends (or decompression sickness) and the seasonal cyclones contributed to staggering mortality rates.

Other relationships were more mutual and productive. Around Twofold Bay near Eden in New South Wales, whalers drew on the traditional knowledge of Yuin people, including their totemic and spiritual connections with killer whales, and several members of the fleet were Aboriginal. Despite the incursions on their fisheries and communities, Indigenous peoples also adapted to the new technologies and markets of colonial society. In many cases, fishing enabled Aboriginal communities to subsist and maintain important cultural and kinship connections, since groups from more arable or urban areas were forced off country and moved to coastal reserves – like Lake Tyers in Victoria, as well as Wreck Bay, Wallaga Lake and La Perouse in New South Wales.

Aboriginal people in these communities drew upon traditional knowledges as well as availing themselves of new methods and equipment. Boats, nets and fishing gear were sometimes supplied to Aboriginal communities along the New South Wales coast. Metal hooks were particularly popular for their durability, noted the Quaker missionary, James Backhouse, who described how Aboriginal fishers along the Shoalhaven River in 1837 used hooks 'formed of pieces of shell, but they preferred English ones, of steel'.

These communities fished for subsistence when other sources of food were literally fenced off, and they traded fish with local non-Indigenous people for items such as flour and tea. Some also publicly shared their Indigenous knowledge, providing a burgeoning tourist trade with images of traditional fishing and hunting, as well as fishing tours, which became a vital way of preserving Indigenous culture, autonomy and financial security.

The fishing pressures on First Nations people around Australia reflected the wider impact of the industry. Fishing for the most part was small scale, local and pre-industrial – a cottage industry. But, by the early 1800s, local fisheries near a now rapidly growing Sydney, such as Port Jackson and Botany Bay, were already seeing the effects of overfishing. One fishing practice involved netting off entire tidal flats at high tide and trapping everything behind a thin layer of fine mesh when the water retreated. Fishers then picked out the larger fish for market, but piles of small fish and fry were simply left to rot.

The next generation of seafood was literally being wiped out before it could reproduce or be harvested. In a paper in 1870 about the fisheries of New South Wales, Alexander Oliver noted how 'The net of the fishermen gradually increased in length, and the meshes decreased in width, so that nothing escaped.' He described how 'bushels upon bushels of small fry – the young of the very best fishes – were left on the beaches after every haul of the seine'. A year later, in 1871, the *Sydney Mail and New South Wales Advertiser* declared that 'the abundance with which we have been blessed . . . seems to have created an impression that our command of fish was inexhaustible'.

There were increasing calls for greater regulation and fisheries management. Fish 'are followed up every creek and cranny by their relentless human enemies' and 'perpetually harassed and hunted' reported the 1880 Commission of Inquiry into the New South Wales Fisheries. It was an anxiety over stocks and sustainability that sounds eerily familiar today.

In an 1883 study, Tenison-Woods described the ailing fishery in Sydney Harbour as 'now scarcely regarded as a source of supply at all'. What's more, he continued, 'this is owing not so much to the pollution of its waters by the sewage of a large city, or their constant disturbance by the traffic of innumerable vessels, as to the ceaseless and often wanton process of netting to which every bay and flat has been subjected for the past fifteen years or twenty years'.

Such dilemmas were not unique. By the late nineteenth century, there was concern around the world, particularly in Britain and Europe, about overfishing. Signs of depletion were everywhere. From the 1860s, colonial governments around Australia tried desperately to regulate the unregulated: who could fish, when and how.

If they didn't, there'd be no fish left for anyone else.

A tangle of scrub reaches across from both banks, almost meeting in the middle above the narrow creek high up in the central plateau of Lutruwita-Tasmania. It's full of fish – grayling and galaxias, mostly – but new neighbours are on their way. A horse traipses down the rocky slopes to the creek and a rider unbuckles his saddlebag.

He pulls out an old billycan and walks over to the creek's edge, gently tipping it out into the cool water. Its precious contents swim off, oblivious to the fact they're changing the course of Australia's natural world forever.

CHAPTER 4

'TROUT WILL EAT ANYTHING BUT THE LOG FENCES' OLD FISH IN A NEW WORLD

'What a dreary land would this be to good old Izaak Walton,' one disappointed correspondent wrote in the *Yeoman and Australian Acclimatiser* in 1863, referring to the seventeenth-century English writer who wrote *The Compleat Angler*. Another writer, Horace William Wheelwright, similarly maligned the fishing in Australian waters: 'One thing is quite clear – that Victoria is no country for the angler,' he penned disparagingly in his *Natural History Sketches* in 1871. 'I hardly ever saw a stream on this side adapted to throwing the fly.'

Given the great quantities of fish in Australia during the nineteenth century and the enviable success of those who fished its coastal and inland waters, their comments seem pretty disingenuous. Indigenous fishers and colonists were making colossal catches in both salt and fresh water around the continent, begging the question: which pond had Wheelwright and others been peering into?

Of course, such scathing attitudes towards Australian angling weren't about the number of fish, but the species available and the ways they could be caught. Seine-netting in Sydney Harbour or propping up meshes across the Tamar weren't quite the 'gentlemanly arts' these writers had in mind. Flicking flies across streams in the Scottish Highlands is more what they imagined.

These fishos were simply homesick. Faced with foreignness, they wanted to make Australia a little more like the world they'd left behind. 'It is not difficult to imagine the sense of alienation experienced by the early Australian settlers,' Bob Dunn wrote in his 1991 book *Angling in Australia: Its History and Writings*. 'They were confronted with a land which bore little resemblance to the one from which they'd come.'

So, the pining colonists set up acclimatisation societies to introduce all the fish species they hankered after. These societies were like gentlemen's clubs and were established to recreate the aristocratic pursuits of home, such as game hunting and fly-fishing. Australian fauna didn't quite cut it as sporting prey, apparently.

All sorts of animals were introduced in an attempt to recreate the leisurely field sports of the colonists' mother country. Deer, foxes and rabbits were brought over, along with great batches of trout and salmon eggs, in an attempt to establish local populations. And the acclimatisers, like acclimatisation advocate Arthur

Nicols, seemed more than happy to wear the costs of the odd miscalculation. 'If they have made a mistake here and there, and have introduced an unmitigated pest like the rabbit, they will one day find compensation in stalking the red deer and bringing the lordly salmon to grass among picturesque granitic hills,' he wrote in 1882. This nostalgic Eden, he hoped, 'may well recall to the eye of the sportsman many a wild scene in the highlands of bonnie Scotland or the softer glories of the Irish lakes'.

It probably goes without saying that Nicols is talking about the pink-fleshed Atlantic variety of salmon, here, not the Australian species – which is a type of herring but was named 'salmon' because it looked vaguely similar. (Don't even get me started on the naming conventions of Australian fish!)

Getting the 'lordly salmon' over to Australia wasn't all that easy, however. Given its cool climate and plentiful fresh-water systems, Tasmania was deemed the obvious destination. It might have been similarly 'bonnie' and 'soft', but it was an awfully long way from England.

The first attempts to transport salmon to Tasmania in the mid-nineteenth century were confounded by the very distance that acclimatisation sought to overcome. On one occasion, unfertilised eggs died before they arrived, when water circulating around the ova became too warm as the ships sailed through the tropics. On another, the carefully packed eggs were spoiled when the ice protecting their boxes melted away en route.

But the Old World advocates were a determined bunch, Nicols insisted. 'The Australasian colonies fortunately possess acclimatisation societies directed by men of ability and energy, who have left nothing undone to establish in the New World the most desirable animal colonists from the old.'

After successive failures, the determined importers devised a system to keep fertilised eggs cool during the long journey. In 1863, 5000 salmon and trout ova were gently placed in wooden boxes filled with moss. These were bedded down with a generous quilt of insulating sawdust, surrounded by ice. Then they were shipped off to Australia on the fastest ocean clipper they could lay their hands on.

Three months later, the precious load (minus some salmon ova delivered to Melbourne) was ferried up the Derwent River and deposited into a local, custom-built salmon pond, where the eggs successfully hatched.

The salmon were released, but never returned from their sea journey – to the bitter disappointment of the Tasmanian Acclimatisation Society. The brown trout, on the other hand, were destined for bigger things. After enough fish had hatched and gone on to spawn themselves, acclimatisers made the next crucial step in establishing the gentle art of fly-fishing in their new world.

Society members trekked across Tasmania by horse and on foot, hauling cans filled with water and baby trout, and released countless little fingerlings into the cool inland Tasmanian creeks and lakes. The first 'liberation' was made in 1866 and, by 1872, there were also populations established in New South Wales, Victoria and New Zealand. Other shipments of brown trout, as well as rainbow trout and brook trout, followed over the next few decades.

More than simply a remedy for homesickness, acclimatisation offered possibilities for economic development and industry. It was thought by some advocates that trout would prosper in and improve the creeks of central Victoria, for example, that had been badly degraded by the throngs of gold miners, who had carved out the banks and soiled the water in search of prosperity. It would be a sort of ecological aquaculture, they suggested, where fisheries damaged by pollution and environmental degradation could be restocked with tougher species, like trout, returning the creeks to some sort of piscatorial productivity.

It wasn't just a hankering for British livestock that pushed the acclimatisation bandwagon, either. As well as species such as brown trout and European lobster, Quinnat (or Chinook) salmon and rainbow trout from North America were also on lists to bring over to Australia. Then there were intercolonial species, such as the Tasmanian giant freshwater crayfish and the New South Wales rock oyster – both slated for importation to Victoria. It was hoped that the introduction and acclimatisation of such creatures could bring in a new era of fisheries development.

By the early twentieth century, however, it was clear that trout was the main attraction for recreational fisheries. Unlike in Britain, the fashion for fly-fishing wasn't indicative of a stunning growth in an Australian aristocracy. Far from it.

In colonial Australia, fishing had been the sport of the 'everyman' since convicts first supplemented their meagre rations with fish (and that expectation that anyone should be able to go fishing has persisted since). Australian workers had gained some of the highest living wages and legislated leisure time anywhere in the world, which meant they had both the time and the money to spend on tourism and holidays. Around the country, newly built railways radiated out across the landscape, and car ownership, albeit restricted to a wealthy few, slowly expanded. Modern transport brought previously remote areas within reach for many ordinary people.

Australia's tourist industry, including fishing, grew accordingly. And, by the early 1900s, the Snowy River was rated by some as a world-class fishery. It was also accessible to anyone who could get there. While recreational fisheries in Britain were restricted to private, wealthy landowners, this was trout fishing with a decidedly 'communitarian character', as sociologist Adrian Franklin described it in 'Performing Acclimatisation: The Agency of Trout Fishing in Australia'. Australian angling represented not class elevation and distinction, but equal access – a more 'equal kind of society'.

What's more, that democratic flavour of Australian trout fisheries continued to expand with each liberation of tiny trout into the rocky creeks, rivers and lakes across Tasmania and the mainland. By 1896, trout fry had been released in eighty-six streams around New South Wales alone. In 1910, that amounted to 38,000 liberations. Sixteen years later, a whopping 525,100 trout were distributed across that state.

Australian trout fishing was becoming so widespread that fishing organisations were established across Tasmania, New South Wales and Victoria in an attempt to regulate the industry and ensure trout's future viability. Groups such as the New South Wales Rod Fishers' Society (formed in 1904) and the Victorian Trout Fishers' Association (formed in 1906 and later renamed as the Victorian Fly Fishers' Association) responded to increasing popular pressure on the burgeoning trout fisheries.

These groups established hatcheries and lobbied for increased fisheries management (including efforts to legally restrict the use of nets in the Derwent River, which caused much resentment among local fishermen, both commercial and recreational). Critically, trout-fishing societies and the fisheries they represented were open to all. It seemed that fly-fishing itself was beginning to acclimatise to Australian conditions.

Just as the trout fishers developed a distinctly Australian temperament and culture, so did the fish, apparently. Rather than sportingly taking to artificial flies, as their ancestors had done in the colonists' home countries with predictable regularity, these ones were much more fickle.

In his description in 1880 of the fish's 'disinclination to take the artificial fly', fishing writer William Senior dismissed the Tasmanian trout as 'by comparison with his ancestors in the old country, a degenerate individual'. The 'poor spirit the fish exhibits when hooked' also demonstrated a reluctance to be caught. Even worse was its supposed taste – 'the crowning evidence of degeneracy', concluded the disappointed Senior, is that 'they are rough and muddy-flavoured for table purposes'.

The trout might have even exceeded the aims of the societies that introduced them, with the fish becoming so acclimatised they were barely recognisable to those the acclimatisers remembered from 'home'. Fishers had to adjust their practices and expectations accordingly. Local anglers realised 'that the trout had changed their habits and behaviour', wrote Franklin in relation to the Tasmanian fish. Some of them developed a sea-running habit (sea trout), or the habit of living mostly in river estuaries (slob trout), which might have been a special adaptation to drought or summer conditions in some waters. 'The trout had begun to do something new in Tasmania that was neither known about or anticipated,' he explained.

Consequently, the practice of fly-fishing had to evolve. Fishers tested new artificial flies that mimicked local insect life, and, given the different climatic conditions in Australia, they had to learn anew the best times to fish in terms of the prevalence of insects, and their life cycles, since fishers would need to mimic their presentation to the trout. It also depended on water levels and water temperature, which can fluctuate according to climatic as well as seasonal trends. And they had to develop new techniques to accommodate the landscape they were fishing in. The degree of difficulty casting flies along steep rocky banks through stands of overgrown acacia is renowned among trout fishers. Grassy fen it is not!

Trout might have demanded a new set of angling nous, but their acclimatisation has been so successful that they are now endemic across Tasmania and mainland Australia. And a century or so after the early trials and disappointments trying to catch these capricious creatures, their place in Australian recreational fishing has become so central they were even honoured with a naturalisation ceremony in Cooma in 1988.

Trout are exciting fish to catch – even a tiddler will put up a great fight – and they're highly regarded as sportfish by anglers. Their value to the recreational fishing and tourism industries is such that state fisheries departments fund hatcheries and restocking programs in lakes and waterways across the country. Nowadays, the fisher's dilemma isn't simply what to catch, as writer and poet Douglas Stewart once asked in his book *Fishing Around the Monaro*, but how to 'fish the evening rise and turn up in time for dinner'?

Yet, the consequences of these ravenous fish became apparent very quickly. A 1905 edition of the *Sydney Morning Herald* quoted an angler as saying that trout 'will eat anything but the log fences hereabout. They have cleared out the bream, the cod, and the carp, but we will not mind that if they stay themselves.'

Trout may be fine table fish and loads of fun to catch, but they hunt a wide range of animals, including aquatic insects, crustaceans, frogs, molluscs and worms, as well as insects that fall on the water surface. They also devour the native fish that prompted their introduction in the first place: the success of trout has been at the expense of fish such as native perch and galaxias (which are now endangered in some places).

Trout's insatiable appetite and penchant for destruction prompted the ecologist Susan Lawler to call them 'rabbits of the river'. 'Obviously, trout fishing is an important part of the tourism industry and many rivers are so well stocked with trout that there is no point in trying to remove them,' she acknowledged in her article in *The Conversation* in 2013. At the same time, however, 'trout are threatening native fish in rivers, impoundments and lakes, and too few people are concerned because they think that trout belong here'.

Some contemporary environmental activists even demanded trout's naturalisation certificate be taken away. And, in a few rivers in the Alpine National Park in Victoria, programs to destock trout are underway in an effort to protect pockets of local fish species.

After 150 years, the acclimatisation project might just have been a little too successful, it seems.

OLD FISH IN A NEW WORLD

Few can refute the thrill of catching a thrashing rainbow trout in the fast-running cold water of a mountain stream, hauling it up onto the bank and then onto the coals for dinner. But what's the cost? (If they could talk, certain species of native fish might beg to differ, for a start.)

Introduced species, such as trout, deer, rabbits and the humble cane toad, were all brought to Australia with great fanfare. Some were introduced to provide game for hunting and nutritional supplements for farmers. Other species came with promises of eradicating pests and boosting economic growth. But many of the imports came with significant strings attached.

Fish introductions alone have completely changed Australia's inland waterways. In Victoria, the stocking of carp began as early as 1859 and, in 1865, in New South Wales, the earliest known introductions occurred near Sydney. In the early 1900s, fingerlings were used to establish several wild populations of carp around Sydney, including in Prospect Reservoir (where they still persist).

In the 1960s, carp were introduced for aquaculture purposes into several farm dams near Mildura, but they escaped following floods. They've become endemic right through the Murray–Darling river system and are a biological nightmare. It's now illegal in New South Wales to return a live carp to the water once caught and annual 'carp bashes' and 'carp kills' have replaced the mountains of Murray cod that locals used to catch.

Trout species have similarly ravaged the cool inland waters of south-eastern Australia and parts of Western Australia. Several native fish species, such as galaxia, Macquarie perch and grayling, all struggle to compete with this ravenous intruder. But the recreational trout fishery is also a vital and valuable part of Australia's economy for recreational anglers, generating significant tourism and recreational spending as well as longstanding cultural connections to the waterways where people fish for them.

Click on the trout pages of government fisheries authorities, and while trout is rightly heralded as a great sportfish, its environmental cost doesn't seem to figure. Trout hatchlings are still released annually by fisheries authorities, and state revenues depend on the availability of trout for recreational anglers. Trout's rapaciousness in local waterways might be a case of unintended consequences, but there's no going back now.

The whistle blows, valves open with a whoosh of steam, and the large paddle starts. Round and round it goes, slowly at first, before picking up speed down the river. The steamer navigates a weekend flotilla of working riverboats and pleasure craft, chugs out across Moreton Bay then veers east towards the open ocean. It heads on past the northern tip of North Stradbroke Island, pushing through the waves and spray. Then it slows.

Near Flat Rock, the anchor drops, the engine quietens and the great paddle finally stops turning; the boat starts to pitch and roll, rather sickeningly, with the swell. Boxes of bait are placed at regular intervals along the deck. The whistle blows again and a boatload of happy punters plop down their lines and wait for the distinctive jag and strike of a hungry snapper.

CHAPTER 5

'NO FISH WILL FIGHT MORE STUBBORNLY' THE ANGLERS

By the early twentieth century, festive fishing outings had become commonplace among leisure seekers from the larger Australian cities along the east coast. Trips departed every weekend from places like Brisbane, Sydney and Newcastle. And you could buy your tickets, for day or overnight trips, from local tackle shops.

The only downside was the seasickness (or 'discharging cargo' as it was fondly called at the time). Running a close second were the sharks, who had a nose for fishing carnage and regularly forced rowdy tour groups to up anchor and head to another bommie.

Snapper Clubs (or 'Schnapper', as the fish were called at the time) chartered whole boats, which regularly steamed out to the various fishing grounds off the coast. Guests lined the gunwales and dropped their lines down below. 'Goodness knows what the fish thought,' wondered writer and avid fisho James Thornton-Champley in his 1912 description of a snapper party. Perhaps they 'thought it was raining squid'. Prizes were doled out for the first fish, the biggest and the most caught on the trip.

In a way, 'recreational fishing' has existed for as long as people have fished: a dead snapper is a dead snapper, whether snared on shellfish hook 900 years ago or hoisted onto a tour boat in 1910. Who's to say catching a feed doesn't generate the same 'fun' and 'rush' reccies get with catch-and-release today? And is there any reason why subsistence fishing, which many people continue to rely on in Australia, isn't also a form of escapism or meditation?

Can we be certain if fishers today feel the same sense of excitement and thrill as those from hundreds of generations ago? It's difficult to make declarative generalisations about how fishing feels across centuries, because those feelings are sensed within our own bodies and in our own times.

While teasing out those different forms of fishing isn't always easy at a personal level, something clearly happened around the turn of the twentieth century to fishing in Australia and elsewhere. Recreational fishing became an industry.

With the advent of the eight-hour work day in the late nineteenth century (thanks to the activism of the union movement), living wages had become higher and were legislated by government. Workers had both increased disposable income and the free time in which to spend it. Primary education had also been compulsory in most Australian colonies as far back as the 1870s, and this meant more people were literate. Increasingly during this time, we see tackle shops advertising their wares in the daily papers, knowing that the punters would be able to read them.

Leisure was now a commodity, and fishing was no exception.

It was also around this time that Australia and its natural world became a focus for local interest and enjoyment. By 1888, 70 per cent of the non-Indigenous population was Australian born. Unlike their parents or grandparents, they had Australian interests and sensibilities. They saw the landscape around them as familiar, rather than something to overcome. The bush and the beach could be revelled in, rather than feared.

The 'native-born' didn't see Australia as foreign, and their fishing matched that local perspective. They didn't simply want to catch acclimatised fish brought in from the old world. They wanted to catch their own.

'No fish will put up a gamer fight,' Thornton-Champley wrote of bream, his favourite little fighter, 'no fish will fight more stubbornly to the bitter end; and very few, if any, exceed him as a table fish.'

By the time the zoologist, keen angler and prolific writer Frederick Aflalo visited Australia from Britain in the late nineteenth century, the fishing scene was well and truly established. 'The favourite sport, bar racing, in the Australian capitals is unquestionably angling,' he declared in his book *A Sketch of the Natural History of Australia*.

Consequently, there was a demand for Australian fishing guides, rather than for the numerous books about British and

European fish filled with advice on how to catch them. People wanted to go down to the local beach, pier or rock ledge and have a fish after work. They didn't want to read about fishing in some far away mythical 'home' that they'd never visited.

In 1895, Charles Thackeray published *The Amateur Fisherman's Guide* to angling in and around Sydney, justifying the project in those terms exactly. 'There have been scores of books written on fishing,' he explained, 'but I have long looked vainly for one of local use.' Guides like Thackeray's give a terrific sense of this burgeoning attitude, which translated into the droll, laconic writing style recognisable in rec-fishing publications to this day.

There was obvious enjoyment and daring in the first flourishes of Australian fishing writing. And you can see the beginnings of a rec-fishing scene that was local, practical and adventurous. Most importantly, it wasn't above having fun.

Writers like Thackeray pondered the art of fishing, with a healthy dose of irony and self-deprecation. 'I am not in a position to state whether a fish experiences untold agonies after being gently removed from the water by a hook through its bony lip,' he penned in his guide, 'but I can unquestionably assert that the fisherman suffers much tribulation when a leatherjacket or tailer [tailor] bites his line and clears off with his hook.'

The texts also show that, while fishing fostered the sort of blokey larrikinism that still characterises much of its writing today, women were also active and visible. Despite the gendered title of *The Amateur Fisherman's Guide*, the book itself suggests recreational fishing was rather more democratic and diverse. 'The gentle sex find the gentle art very pleasant,' Thackeray

LEISURE, TOURISM AND THE OUTDOORS

By the end of the nineteenth century, Australia had been colonised for one hundred years and the Australian-born were forging a new Australian, rather than British, identity. The famous periodical, *The Bulletin*, proselytised this new breed of Australian who turned his or her nose up at the old world and looked towards the Australian bush for inspiration. Artists of the Heidelberg School, including painters Tom Roberts, Arthur Streeton and Frederick McCubbin, similarly found inspiration in the world around them and viewed the landscape as comforting and familiar, rather than foreign.

It wasn't just a matter of writers and artists romanticising the Australian bush. In day-to-day life, there was also a growing sense that the outdoors could provide sustenance and salvation in the form of recreation for an increasingly urban population. Australians went to the beach and took up bushwalking, camping, bird watching and fishing as outlets from bustling modern life. Gazetted in 1879, the Royal National Park, just south of Sydney, was the second national park in the world to be established; it reflected the idea that the Australian bush was important enough to be protected and enjoyed, rather than simply to be conquered.

However, it was no accident that this burgeoning interest in the Australian landscape coincided with the end of frontier wars – in the southern parts of Australia, in particular, surviving Indigenous communities had mostly been moved off their country and onto missions, reserves and stations by the turn of the twentieth century. 'The bush', much of it now emptied of its original owners, became a place that non-Indigenous people increasingly understood as 'safe' and something they attached themselves to as they sought to carve out a distinctively Australian identity.

admitted. Women took part in fishing competitions and fishing outings, and at least one Sydney tackle shop was run by a woman – a Mrs Christensen, who advertised her wares in Thackeray's guide.

In 1821, Elizabeth Macquarie, wife of the Governor of New South Wales, famously out-fished her husband in Watsons Bay when they were unexpectedly camped there for an evening and often participated in both boat and shore-based fishing expeditions. There are plenty of images from the time that show fishing was a communal leisure activity that everyone could enjoy, with local newspapers depicting scenes of whole families out on boats fishing together, or sitting on the banks of local waterways, rods in hand. These windows into the past confirm that even in early colonial society, fishing was a form of inclusive recreation and pleasure.

As well as tackle-shop ads and humorous musings, fishing guides also published detailed information about how and where to catch fish. They provided maps and descriptions of special spots around the larger centres like Sydney and Melbourne, as well as bus, tram and ferry timetables and information about boat hire and walking tracks.

The guide writers wrote about what tackle to buy and what knots to tie. They recommended remedies for common injuries (apparently, the flesh of an onion was essential in any tackle bag to 'alleviate the pain' of being spiked by a flathead or catfish, or to soothe the agonising sting of a fortescue spine).

And they described in great detail the bait preferences of Australian fish, which wouldn't sound out of place in a fishing magazine today. Want to catch drummer? Slice open a cunjevoi and fix the tougher portions of the flesh onto the hook. Are you going to try and snag a luderick? The bait 'most relished' by these shy fish is sea lettuce. If it's bream you're after, then take the head off a prawn and slide it down the shaft of your hook – tie the bait on with fine wire if you want better purchase. Almost anything will do for snapper fishing – squid, yellowtail, mackerel, lobster, beef, garfish, roast octopus, crabs, cunjevoi, tripe – as long as it's fresh. Fancy a barra? You can't go wrong with live bait.

What distinguishes the era was the technology available to fishers. Rods could be as low key as a long stick with string on the end. At the fancier end of the market, punters weren't debating the merits of the latest carbon or fibreglass blank, but choosing between hickory, whale bone or split cane. Simple wooden or brass reels could be bought cheaply from any local tackle shop, or they weren't used at all. Fishing line was made from cotton, flax or hemp – natural fibres that tended to rot quickly in salt water and snapped easily since they didn't have the same stretch or durability of modern synthetics – or silk thread. The latest hi-tech leader wasn't some superior Japanese monofilament, but line painstakingly extracted (sucked by mouth, no less!) from the gut sacs of silkworm larvae.

There was no GPS, four-wheel drive or outboard to get you to that special spot. Fishers took a ferry, or they rowed or hiked in. Rusting steel hooks were kept in service with endless coatings of vaseline. (The mass-produced soft plastic lures that fish find irresistible, and that now dominate the market, were at least a century away.) And, to compensate for the thick, unresponsive lines, fishers rubbed their fingertips with pumice or sandpaper, which kept them primed to feel the faintest nibble of a timid bream at night.

Berley didn't come as pre-frozen bombs or dry pellets and didn't include specially scented oils. It was usually some ghastly homemade concoction, 'a pungent groundbait composed of bran, condemned tinned salmon, salt herrings, and cheese', as Aflalo described in painful detail in *A Sketch of the Natural History of Australia*. 'The attractions of a conglomeration of these ingredients, as carefully blended as those of a Madras curry, need no eulogy. They will be readily imagined.'

But, when you read Thackeray's description of bream fishing, it's clear that, apart from the actual gear, very little has changed. There 'is an exquisite pleasure in manipulating a slender thread of silk to its extreme tension with the pull of a 3 lb black bream', he extolled in *The Amateur Fisherman's Guide*. When I read that excerpt, I'm right there with him, desperately navigating the bream over the rocks and kelp, despite the century between us. Thackeray could just as easily be describing a catch from yesterday.

Descriptions of rock fishing at the turn of the twentieth century similarly set your heart racing. In his account of the Sydney fishing scene, Aflalo noted (with some relish) the precarious descents and near-misses of these committed anglers. 'The rock-fishers face the most appalling climbs, scrambling to their favourite grounds over all but perpendicular faces of slippery rock,' he wrote, heart in mouth. Aflalo described fishers 'creeping along ledges a few inches broad, from which a single false step would plunge them among the sharks a hundred feet below'.

The thrill and excitement that comes through in early writings of a century ago are exactly what motivates rock fishers today. It 'can be almost always regarded as fast and furious, especially when a man casts his line into a school of squire [snapper], tailer [tailor], or rock-cod', wrote Thackeray in his 1895 guide. Although it was high-stakes fishing, with plenty of snags and lost trophies. The 'rock fisherman has unfortunately a large vocabulary of expletives', he also admitted.

The danger of the sport was readily apparent back then – and part of its attraction. Aflalo was characteristically dramatic in his description of a rock fishing trip in the late 1800s near the precipitous headlands of Sydney Harbour. 'Accidents occur now and again,' he acknowledges, 'and you may find that the ledge you are fishing from has acquired a flavour of historic association from such local names as "Brown's Fall" or "Smith's Mistake"!'

Although the locals were much more nonchalant, Aflalo notes, 'Familiarity breeds contempt; and I have seen Sydney youths trip to and from these fishing-grounds with no more care than they would up Pitt Street.' More perplexing for Aflalo was the fact that those risk-takers endangered their lives for luderick, wirrah and Australian salmon, fish that he derided as 'ill-flavoured' and 'insipid'.

For everyone else, it was the sport, as much as the eating, that drew them in. Rock fishing camps were dotted along the coast, with pots and camping gear stuffed behind bushes on clifftops and among the sand dunes, awaiting the next evening fishing sortie or weekend escape.

The more adventurous anglers went further afield, buying tickets on intercolonial steamers that plied their trade on the shipping lane between Melbourne and Sydney. About halfway, they'd get dropped off onto the waiting boats of the lighthouse keepers from nearby Montague Island, who'd take them back to camp and fish on their remote, exposed rocks. 'It is not a trip for those who are fearsome or sea sick, or very fond of luxurious surrounds,' says Thackeray in *The Amateur Fisherman's Guide*.

Those rocks were perilous, but fishers dragged in some spectacular catches from them, even in the middle of the larger urban centres. Blue groper of around 40 to 50 pounds (18 to 23 kilograms) were commonly caught handlining in and around Sydney during the early nineteenth century, while lobsters were hauled up by the dozen near Bondi Beach.

Along the entire coast and in the rivers of the inland, anglers pulled up loads of enormous fish. 'It matters not, when the fish are about, whether you have one or ten hooks on your line, you can catch a fish on each hook,' wrote John Cameron in astonishment, describing a fishing party to Flat Rock off Moreton Bay, Queensland, in 1888 in his book *The Fisherman: A Guide to the Inexperienced*. 'It is a wonderful sight to see the deck of a steamer bestrewed with hundreds of these grand fish.' Today, this scene of bounty probably seems like sheer excess, but it's an indication of just how many fish there were back then, as well as revealing a lack of knowledge about the sustainability of those fisheries.

The anglers

On the Macleay River in New South Wales, commercial fisherman Pat Clifford remembered catching great hauls of prawns using a chaff bag when he was only five or six years old in the early twentieth century.

Murray cod commonly tipped the scales at 25 pounds (11 kilograms), and catches upward of 100 pounds (45 kilograms) weren't unusual. In 1902, three bridge workers reportedly pulled a cod up from the Barwon River, near Walgett in New South Wales, that weighed a whopping 250 pounds (113 kilograms), after they were woken one night by a huge commotion in the water. Apparently, the men fashioned a rig from a large hook and some old fencing wire, then baited it with a lump of bloody kangaroo meat, before fixing it to a stake on the muddy riverbank.

It's hard not going green with envy reading fishing accounts from the past. 'Fish O! all alive O! is heard, first from the bow, and in the stern, then all over the ship, and a squabble takes place as to which did catch the first fish,' Cameron recalled in his 1888 account of a trip to Flat Rock. But 'everyone is so busily engaged with his line in the actual work of fishing, that no one bothers his head for the time being, as to who did land the "phenomenon"'.

A party of seven near Caloundra in Queensland bagged 516 snapper in an hour and a half in the 1890s. In 1894, the *Brisbane Telegraph* reported a catch of 1060 snapper in five hours by a group of eight fishing off the Tweed River. And in 1905, eight fishers nabbed over a hundred snapper just east of Flat Rock, in an hour.

It wasn't just mighty bounties of trophy fish that kept fishers content. The humble bream and flattie were much celebrated among fishers out on the water and around the dinner table: 'Many's the time, and oft, the Flathead has saved the angler from returning empty-handed. Summer or winter, he has kept the pan from growing rusty,' wrote Thornton-Champley in *Australian Angler's Guide and Sea Fisher's Manual* in 1910.

According to angling writer Bob Dunn, it wasn't unusual for five hundred people to be sitting on the banks of the Maribyrnong River in Melbourne in the early 1900s waiting for the bream run. The last time I kayaked there in the early 2000s the only 'fish' I saw were an old suitcase and a shopping trolley. While an extensive rehabilitation program is now underway and attempting to rebuild habitat for native fish, the recent floods in 2022 demonstrate the challenges of environmental restoration in urban waterways.

Sometimes the pursuit was as much about subsistence and survival as the thrill of the chase. There are accounts of Aboriginal people rock fishing near Sydney with tackle and handlines supplied by the colonists as early as the 1830s. A century later, during the Great Depression, scores of unemployed men (and sometimes their wives and families, too) occupied shanty fishing communities right around the Australian coast. Their huts were built from anything at hand – chiselled into sandstone cliffs, fashioned from driftwood, sheets of old corrugated iron, or flattened kerosene tins. There they camped out on the fringes of settlement, living off fish and other seafood, while selling or bartering their excess catch for supplies.

Such accounts perhaps blur the definition of 'rec-fishing', but they don't detract from the extraordinary picture of angling in Australia before industrialisation and mass urbanisation. Like the early days of Australia's commercial fisheries, these stories describe catches we can only dream of today – despite the technological advances at our fingertips. If they were catching that many fish by literally dropping a line in the water, just how many fish were there?

But that bounty couldn't last with the fishing pressures exerted by a growing population. The writings that reveal so much about Australia's fishing largesse also heralded deep concerns about noticeable decreases in fish populations as well as the future of fisheries.

Even by the turn of the twentieth century, there was concern about declining stocks for rec-fishers. 'Originally Port Jackson was an angler's paradise,' noted Thornton-Champley, 'but the vicinity of a great city, and the accompanying demand for fresh fish, has depleted the once seemingly illimitable supply.'

Fishing tours had to go further and further out to sea, away from the populated coastal hubs, as fishing grounds were flogged in quick succession. Huge snapper were still plentiful in Sydney Harbour in the 1850s, but by 1895 steamers were heading to offshore reefs and up to Broken Bay to track down these fish. By the 1890s, some Brisbane fishers had to travel as far as the Tweed River for a decent catch.

Tensions arose in the fishing community between the recreational and commercial industries. Both called on the government for increased regulation and research. To make their case heard, rec-fishers gathered to form alliances that lobbied local and federal governments.

The Amateur Fishermen's Association of New South Wales was founded in 1895 and was instrumental in gaining state government support to close a large part of Port Hacking, in Sydney's south, to commercial fishing in 1902. The New South Wales Rod Fishers' Society and the Amateur Fishermen's Association of Queensland were both founded in 1904 and represented alliances that supported the interests of rec-fishers.

Along with royal commissions into the fishing industry conducted by colonial governments in the late nineteenth century, lobbying by these rec-fishing peak bodies influenced the imposition of fisheries management by government. Regulations such as catch limits, closed seasons and size restrictions were enforced in fisheries around the country in the early twentieth century.

Yet questions about the future of fishing remained. Could the health of stocks be maintained? Could commercial and recreational industries coexist? Could government ensure the simple pleasure of an afternoon fishing for generations to come?

They're questions that continue to be asked to this day.

The engine's running and its gentle throb can be felt through the humming deck. Filleting knives are neatly lined up by the cutting boards near the ship's bow, and someone's hosing off the blood from this morning's catch. There's a constant and slightly acrid smell of old fish.

In the centre of the deck is a little hatch with a lid. Inside, a steel ladder drops down to the icy hold below. It's dark and filled to the brim with neatly stacked 10-kilogram boxes of fish fillets, snap frozen by the boat's powerful compressor. They sit waiting to be unloaded and taken away by refrigerated truck to the city markets.

CHAPTER 6

'BOOM AND BUST'
MODERN FISHERIES

In the first half of the twentieth century, commercial fishing was still largely a cottage industry undertaken by small communities who harvested locally. For the most part, boats were powered by the wind and the tide, or rowed. Nets, pots and lines were set and hauled in by hand. Transport was haphazard and the national market for fish was patchy and small.

Fast forward fifty years to the latter decades of the twentieth century, and those multimillion-dollar fishing outfits operating in the vast offshore fisheries with their multimillion-dollar licences made these early ventures into industrial fishing look practically palaeolithic.

This 'Great Fishing Leap Forward' happened over a relatively short space of time. Until the 1940s, commercial fishing was pretty rudimentary along the entire logistics chain. From the small boats that worked the inland and coastal waters, to the storage, transport and warehousing of their catch, the fishing industry was mostly local and piecemeal. It wasn't uncommon for fish to be left out in the open for twenty-four to forty-eight hours before being shipped to the Sydney markets and, in some cases, as many as six days went by before the product was sold in town.

Aboriginal commercial fishers at the Wreck Bay community on the New South Wales South Coast were periodically forced to bury whole catches when their trucks got bogged on the dirt tracks leading up to the main road. On the state's Mid North Coast, fisher Dulcie Stace remembered swatting flies off their boxes of prawns with a bunch of leaves while waiting for the train to take the haul down to Sydney in the middle decades of the twentieth century.

In Portland, Victoria, during the 1920s, fishers held their collective breath every time a train with a load of barracouta headed out on the night service to Melbourne – the long way. 'The train from Portland went way up around Ballarat, that was the trouble,' fisherman Roy Patterson recollected. 'They'd be dead two nights before they got sold. No ice, nobody ever iced their fish.'

Even in the 1950s, there were problems with logistics and infrastructure. Colossal fish dumps happened all over the country when fish couldn't be transported or processed in time. A South Australian fisher who worked out of Port Lincoln remembered that 'out of one load we had 37 ton of salmon buried because they couldn't hold them long enough to get them all canned'.

It's no wonder that fish wasn't high on the menu for those Australians who didn't catch their own.

Several royal commissions were held into the state of fisheries and their lack of commercial development in the late nineteenth and early twentieth centuries. They found that demand was a major part of the problem. 'Opinion has been expressed that our people are not a fish-eating community,' noted one New South Wales commission report in 1894. Another, in 1911, found that most Australians exhibited 'a strong prejudice against what are known as common fish, such as mullet, blackfish, tailor, etc. Large numbers of people will not buy these fish.'

What's more, when the fish did get to market, commercial fishers got paltry reward for their work. One fisherman from Western Australia used to sail his catch of snapper from Shark Bay all the way down to Fremantle, over 700 kilometres away, because of the prohibitive costs of transport in the 1930s. The price for freighting them by rail was over a penny a pound, but he was only paid two pennies a pound for the fish, which would have left him with next to nothing.

With transport so expensive and unreliable, fishers simply didn't have the money – or a market share of the food industry – to upgrade their gear and boost their catch. Although, with such low demand and supply, the upshot was that most fisheries weren't yet subject to overexploitation.

In the 1920s, fish in the Victorian bays of Port Welshpool and Port Phillip were so abundant that fishers who were netting during the flathead season took ten to fifteen boxes after only a couple of hours. Barracouta ran so thick that a catch of fifty dozen in an hour from a small, two-person boat was considered poor. Commercial fishers handlining for snapper only had to row out 'a hundred yards' or so, Victorian fisher Len Beazley recollected, and they'd quickly have 'half a dozen snapper just like that'. They didn't even bother longlining in 'those days because there were too many fish'. (I haven't heard that said in a long time!) 'If they went longlining they'd get a snapper on every hook, and they couldn't do anything with them,' Beazley explained, 'nobody wanted 'em.'

With apparently such high stocks but relatively low catches, the commercial fishing industry seemed like a wasted opportunity for government and industry types that were keen to bolster Australian national interests and economic development. If there were so many fish out there to catch, they reasoned, why was the industry so small?

State and federal governments stepped in, pushing the development of commercial fishing in the early decades of the twentieth century. They subsidised canneries and transport infrastructure. They supported research and development, as well as promoting the industry more broadly. The New South Wales Government even established its own trawl industry, importing and building several steam trawlers to work its seemingly bountiful coastal waters. It also developed a network of state fish shops and purpose-built lorries to transport and market the produce in order to boost demand.

If that all sounds a bit like seaside socialism, that's because it sort of was. State and federal governments were keen for the commercial fishing industry to develop, for Australian primary production to increase and diversify. The only way they felt that was possible was through government intervention and ownership.

The inefficiencies and difficulties that had prevented the industry's early development also hampered its collectivisation: the cost of fishing was still greater than the rewards; distances between fisheries and markets were still proving to be a big barrier to commercial expansion; and technology (such as petrol engines and refrigeration) was still costly and unreliable. Eventually, in the 1920s, the New South Wales Government divested its financial interest in the state trawling industry and its fish shops, selling them to private industry.

But that initial state involvement in fisheries did provide the spurt needed for the commercial sector to develop and industrialise. And Australian governments (state and federal) continued to actively support industrial development through fisheries management, research and commercialisation in the 1940s and 1950s. They did so by slinging money and support towards infrastructure projects, research and development into fisheries science and technology, as well as the establishment of fishing cooperatives, in an attempt to expand the industry and its market.

This coincided with the growing popularity of fish and chip shops that boosted demand for fresh fillets in the 1920s. Meanwhile, canneries were also being built in coastal towns around the country as a way of capitalising on the great seasonal schools of Australian salmon.

A community of Aboriginal fishers, as painted by Joseph Lycett in about 1817, spotting from the clifftops, pulling crays out from under rock ledges, spearing in the shallows and cooking a feed on the beach.

(National Library of Australia)

These sculptural-looking rock arrangements are the *Ngunnhu*, ancient fish traps on the Barwon River in Brewarrina, New South Wales. Photographed here in the 1890s, the traps supplied catches that fed local Aboriginal people for thousands of years. (Powerhouse Museum)

FISHING. Nᵒ 2.

Aboriginal fishing prowess – using a fish gig or fizgig spear, as it was often called by the colonists, in waters around what we know as present-day Sydney. (National Library of Australia)

In convict artist Joseph Lycett's painting of Aboriginal night fishing (c. 1817), fish are lured to the side of the canoes by torchlight before being speared, while a catch is cooked up on the shore.

By the late Micky the Cripple Aborigine Ulladulla

Mickey of Ulladulla, located on the South Coast of New South Wales, created a series of extraordinary images from an Indigenous perspective, including this one of Aboriginal and colonial fishing in the late nineteenth century.
(National Library of Australia)

An Aboriginal fisherwoman in her *nowie* – line in the water, paddle at the ready, while a fire is on the go, and a baby lies at her feet. Women were master skippers and skilled line fishers, navigating their canoes across large waterways to provide for their families and communities.
(State Library of New South Wales)

Aboriginal rock art, such as this painting in Kakadu, offers important Indigenous perspectives on fish and fishing in Australia.
(Photo taken by the author)

The bounty of Australia's natural world was often inscribed onto objects and recorded in texts by colonists. This collector's chest from around 1818 reflected that scientific curiosity and was gifted to Governor Macquarie.
(State Library of New South Wales)

FISH MARKET AT WOOLLOOMOOLOO. N. S. W.

In 1875, when this engraving of the Woolloomooloo fish markets was made, ice and refrigeration were not widely used, and the fishing industry consisted of small, localised fishing fleets and distribution methods.

(State Library of Victoria)

Communities of Chinese fish curers popped up all over Australia following the Victorian gold rush in the 1850s, selling preserved fish to Chinese miners working on nearby goldfields. (State Library of New South Wales)

Murray-cod fishermen were known as 'Murray Whalers' because the fish they caught were so enormous. For modern fishers, catches like this one in 1924 would be impossible to believe without archival records. (National Library of Australia)

The allure of angling opened up the bush as a place for relaxation and recreation for many Australian-born and their families, such as this fishing party photographed at the turn of the twentieth century.
(National Library of Australia)

The thrill of the catch. Trout fishing's popularity spurred a whole new tourist industry in Australia, and it continues to be a major drawcard. (State Library of New South Wales)

There's something incredible about fishing underwater – hunting fish in their own environment and seeing the world they inhabit. Spearfishing became an increasingly popular sport in Australia with the availability of goggles, masks and fins in the early twentieth century, and its popularity continues to grow. (State Library of New South Wales)

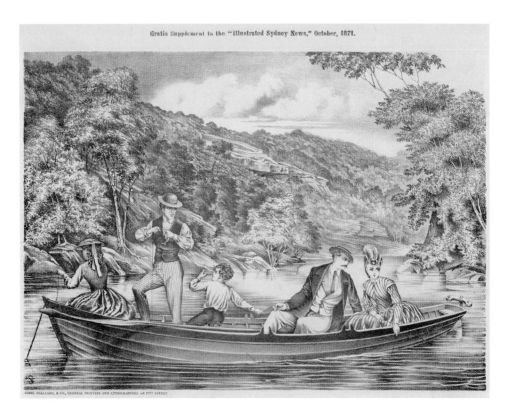

'Fishing, a Sketch in Mossman's Bay, Port Jackson' appeared in the *Illustrated Sydney News* in 1871 and showed that dropping a line in was enjoyed by the whole family.
(National Library of Australia)

Front page news! By the turn of the twentieth century, recreational fishing was one of the most common pursuits in Australia.
(National Library of Australia)

Not all fishing was for fun. During the Great Depression, unemployed men (and sometimes their families) fished for subsistence, camping by rivers and beaches or inhabiting crude shacks, like these cave dwellers did (*top*), along the coast.
(National Library of Australia)

Salmon fishing was a communal affair, as seen in this 1967 photograph by Jeff Carter, with whole communities pitching in to shoot out the nets, haul in the fish and harvest the catch. Salmon canneries dotted the Australian coast during the peak of this fishery.

(© Jeff Carter Archive)

A photo that tells a thousand words: fishers atop a mountain of orange roughy in Portland, Victoria. The image was taken in 1988 when the fishery was on the brink of collapse. (© Ruth Maddison)

Is there anything better than a great catch – for the table or the photo album? Trout (*top left*), whiting (*top right*) and striped marlin (*above*) are just some of the species many get up at dawn for . . .

Fishing continues to be central to Indigenous people's lives and communities around Australia – a way of connecting to Country and culture, as well as spending time with family. (State Library of Western Australia)

An image of a desperate fisho trying to save a fishery in crisis. It's a powerful emblem of some of the environmental challenges fishing faces, but also shows just how passionate people are to step in. (OzFish Unlimited)

Fish restocking and habitat restoration is now one of the key activities of fisheries managers around Australia, often in collaboration with local landholders, fishing clubs and conservation groups. Here, juvenile mulloway are being released into the Georges River in Sydney. (Courtesy of NSW Department of Primary Industries)

You can't get a bigger smile than a fish-photo smile! A smashing Queensland coral trout on a beautiful day.

Modern fisheries

From Shark Bay in Western Australia, to around the south of the Australian continent and as high as northern New South Wales, huge shoals of salmon regularly came right into the coast to feast on baitfish. Whole communities would be waiting for them, and their rusty old tractors would rumble across the sand at the first sight of the salmon soup broiling just offshore. Seine nets were quickly rowed out through the waves and around the school of fish. The towing ropes would be pulled by hand or tied to the old tractors and the fish were hauled up onto the beaches in the bulging nets.

Salmon were ideal for canning because of their high oil content, which meant they stayed relatively moist during the process. Large quantities of dried and preserved fish had been imported into Australia in the late nineteenth and early twentieth centuries, reflecting cultural tastes for northern hemisphere fish such as cod, as well as the poor state of locally caught fish which were difficult to keep fresh. It was hoped that the development of a local canning industry might pick up some of that market.

At the height of the industry's expansion, tons of Australian salmon were brought to the canneries, scaled, then shot down a large chute, where bandsaws whipped off their heads. Then they were finned, gutted and thoroughly cleaned before the cannery conveyor belt took them through an obstacle course of revolving knives. These blades sliced the fish into can-sized cutlets, before the cutlets dropped into a drum of brine.

In his book *Fish and Fisheries of Australia*, T. C. Roughley, a New South Wales Fisheries inspector, described the scene in the Moruya cannery in vivid detail: 'With hands covered with rubber gloves the girls pack the fish into the cans, which are weighed and subjected to careful inspection', before being heated and vacuum-sealed.

I still remember tins of white-fleshed Australian salmon in the supermarket when I was a kid – although they are much maligned as an eating fish, with a firm chewy texture and slightly oily taste, and the last of Australia's fish canneries closed in the 1990s. The only tinned salmon you can buy now is the pink Atlantic variety.

It wasn't just fish that the modern industry developed around. Over in the west, turtle soup and calipash were on the menu, thanks to the hard work of the Western Australian Chief Inspector of Fisheries in the early 1900s, who vigorously promoted the industry's development. Factories sprouted up and down the coast producing gallons of the stuff, along with other 'canned delicacies', the Perth *Daily News* proudly announced.

Despite a 'practically inexhaustible' supply, according to *The West Australian* in 1923, these ventures tended to be short-lived. They succumbed variously to tin shortages caused by the war (which prevented canning), and a market collapse during the Great Depression. But the industry's haphazard approach to quality control also seems to have played a role in its demise. First, there was a suspected, rather scandalous, dilution of the Rockingham turtle soup batch with beef. There were also stories of rather cavalier experimentations with various batches, where the cooks were so drunk that they never wrote down their recipes.

Shark fishing provided another lucrative opportunity for Australia's burgeoning commercial fishing industry. Since shark liver is very high in vitamin A, they were an ideal replacement for the growing vitamin industry following shortages of cod-liver oil due to the expansion of World War II into the North Sea fisheries. In South Australia, fishermen set long lengths of strong sisal rope with multiple hooks off the back of their little boats and caught school sharks by the ton.

I say fisher*men* because they almost always were in those days, even during the war when other primary industries saw an increase in female labour. The physical demands and dangers of daily commercial fishing inevitably led to gender biases in the industry. In the shark fishery, it was the wives who rendered down the livers by hand, in large backyard vats. The putrid stench seeped out over their garden fences to the streets and neighbours beyond. It's hard to say who had the more difficult job.

Government fisheries departments, primary industries and research bodies, such as the Council for Scientific and Industrial Research (CSIR, later renamed CSIRO), all worked towards the expansion of Australian commercial fishing. The burgeoning science of fisheries management went hand in hand with its industrial development in exploiting the vast natural reserves of Australian fish. Research into fishing grounds, stock numbers and marine biology, as well as fish life cycles, hatching and aquaculture, all comprised this government interest and investment in understanding and capitalising on Australia's marine resources.

As it turned out, however, the reserves weren't always all that vast. Compared with the cold, nutrient-rich seas of Europe and North America, Australia's oceans are much less productive. Despite staggering early catches, the unpredictability and insecurity of its fisheries turned out to be more than just casual observation. It didn't take long for concern to arise over the depletion of fishing stocks during the early years of the trawl industry. South of Sydney, tiger flathead mysteriously began disappearing from the trawl catch after only a decade.

So much effort had gone into developing the steam trawler industry in the 1910s and the industry's expansion the following decade. But by the 1930s the depletion of tiger flathead stocks had become apparent. The annual catch rate for tiger flathead per hour of trawling in 1937 was less than half of what was achieved at the beginning of the 1920s. By the 1960s, the fishery had effectively collapsed altogether.

Despite anxiety from some government biologists over these stock depletions, governments and fisheries managers were generally behind the pace in terms of regulation. Some even argued that the stock reductions were the result of naturally occurring fish migrations and fluctuating water temperature, rather than overfishing. The strict guidelines that today's commercial fishers have to deal with regarding catch limits, bycatch (sea animals unintentionally caught in fishing nets), mesh size and fishing zones were decades away.

By the 1960s, the tiger flathead population was only 20 per cent of pre-1915 levels. That it's now only 40 per cent, nearly a century after their initial decline, shows just how much longer it takes fish stocks to recover than to harvest.

With such dramatic reductions, there was pressure from

industry and government fishing agencies to move out of existing fishing zones and work new ones. The question was: which fishery would be exploited next?

Extensive surveys by the CSIR from the late 1930s revealed large unexploited resources of school fish offshore. Although there was some debate about the extent and resilience of these stocks, questions about how to catch them commercially became a fixture in fisheries management discussions. The Australian Government even brought out an American tuna boat in 1950 to trial methods for tuna fishing and to capitalise on the unused stocks of southern bluefin tuna.

It was known that tuna were around – the challenge was how to catch them and what to do with the catch. In the early 1940s, there were complaints in the *Australian Fisheries* magazine that Albany's harbour, in Western Australia, was 'nearly choked' with big tuna, and they had become an embarrassment and a pest to the local net fishermen.

The question of how to deal with these huge quantities of tuna was partly answered by the growing fisheries infra-structure in the form of transport and canneries. It was also aided by big changes in the Australian market. From the end of World War II, thousands of migrants from the Mediterranean swelled the national population. They brought with them skills as tradies, construction workers and fishers; they also brought a taste for the seafood they ate in Europe – like tuna, calamari, pipis and sardines.

Until then, species such as tuna had only ever been caught for bait. Now there was an expanding market for human consumption of the fish. But in order to exploit that resource, the industry needed some large-scale modification, since the fishing boats would be entering high seas, off the continental shelf. They had to be able to cope with smashing southerly busters, as well as have the capacity to move quickly to grounds further out if the fishing was quiet. They needed mechanised winches to haul in the large nets and epically long lines. They needed bigger fuel tanks, more horsepower, safety gear and freezing capacity.

The new gear was durable, but expensive: plastic nets, synthetic lines, fuel and hydraulics all cost money. The large ocean-going rigs had GPS plotters, echo sounders, complex mechanical systems and sometimes even spotting planes. By the 1970s, commercial fishing was moving into an era of large overheads.

Compare these outfits to the rigs they'd fished from only a generation earlier, where most boats were still without engines and the bulk of the work was by hand. Fishing went from backyard businesses to serious companies with serious over-drafts in the space of a few decades.

Encouragement from the Australian Government, along with profitable catch rates and optimistic assessments of resource size and depth, caused a rapid expansion of commercial fish-eries. On shore, commercial growth was similarly impressive. Investments enabled the freezing, filleting and canning infra-structure to process large amounts of fish.

New technology meant fresher fish – transport, markets and fish sellers enabling the capacity to store and move produce quickly. It also resulted in more fish, since fishing boats could be out for longer and, with the large overheads, boats needed higher takings in order to turn a profit. Rather than bringing in their small hauls every day, fishing became a serious industry – with serious catches to match.

Even with the latest modifications, fishing could still be exhilarating. There's nothing quite like the sight of a sea boiling from hundreds of enormous pelagic predators attacking a school of baitfish. Out in the middle of the ocean, with no land in sight, the markers that guide your boat are all unseen – it's the currents, upwellings and submarine topography of seabeds and reefs that indicate where fish aggregate. When they do, spectacularly sometimes, the underwater world becomes something you can also see from above the surface.

Just imagine what it would have been like to run through a school of colossal, churning bluefin tuna standing off the stern of a 15-metre boat. Your bamboo pole has a long wire trace with a hook and feather bobbing enticingly off the back of the boat. Bang! You flick a 20-kilogram fish over your shoulder onto the deck, and drop the lure back in. Bang, bang, bang. One boat in 1950 caught 6 tons of bluefin in just forty minutes.

It was a tuna frenzy . . . until the tuna stocks collapsed. So, the fishers moved on to the next thing – orange roughy. And then the next – gemfish. It was a dangerous and unsustainable cycle of boom and bust.

In the 1951 to 1952 season, the southern bluefin tuna haul was 49 tons; nearly twenty-five years later, in 1974 to 1975, it was a staggering 5227 tons. In 1981 to 1982, catches pipped

3000 tons a year. Two years later, they were crashing fast: in 1983 to 1984, the catch was only 899 tons. Today, after years of protection that has included radically reduced catch limits and the establishment of an international advisory committee to manage the migratory fishery, current global estimates of the southern bluefin tuna population still sit somewhere around 20 per cent of virgin biomass (population density prior to commercial harvesting), although numbers of fish of reproductive age (over ten years) is around 13 per cent. They've consequently become so valuable that it's more cost effective to fly their frozen carcasses to the Tsukiji fish markets in Tokyo as sashimi-grade meat than to process them in Australia.

Inland, the same thing happened with Murray cod, where the fishery peaked just after World War I and then became increasingly unprofitable as the catches declined – first for the larger operators and, in the 1950s and 1960s, for everyone else. In 2001, the New South Wales fishery closed altogether.

Many commercial fishers were concerned: they understood the clear need for restrictions, but they were also wary of what that would entail. In the Gulf of Carpentaria, prawner Ken Tidswell described in 1990 the unsustainability of the industry he was a part of. Trawlers operated 'twenty-four-seven', he explained, with motherships regularly bringing fuel and supplies. 'Of course the fisheries couldn't handle that,' he admitted.

The rapid acceleration of the industry may have made the catches more spectacular, but it didn't make the work any easier. Fishing was, and remains, hard physical labour – whether netting small estuaries in tinnies or wrestling with large ocean catches.

Sure, winches can pull up the fish, and engines can get the boats back to shore, but it's the fishers who drive the winch and set the nets or longlines in rolling swells before dawn. It's the fishers who box and ice the catch in the swaying hold, who fiddle with the flat battery or broken sump in the engine room at 2 am (sometimes during a gale!) and who then back that up with a night watch as the boat motors towards port.

Fishing boats are equipped with radars, EPIRBs and satellite navigation, but they still go down and they still lose fishers overboard. Accidents are common in this exposed and labour-intensive industry. And it's hard to stay afloat in freezing cold water at the best of times, let alone when you're weighed down with heavy waterproof gear in the dark. This is no job for the faint-hearted.

So, it's no surprise that when profits began to take a dive in Australia and the writing was on the wall for overfishing, many commercial fishers took the option of a buy-out. Governments simply had to take control of fish management, otherwise there'd be none left.

Regulation of fisheries grew more prominent from the 1970s, when it became clear that precipitous slumps in fish stocks were following the development of every new fishery. Laws of the sea were revised internationally to facilitate fisheries resource management country by country. National regulations were being drawn up and enforced by state and

'THE STOCKS MARKET'

The history of commercial fishing is a bit like mining: a discovery of great natural resources, a rush to get rich, and then a move on to the next thing, leaving the plundered stocks on the brink of obliteration. In the North Sea it was cod. In the Southern Ocean it was humpback whales. And in Australia it was tiger flathead, southern bluefin tuna, orange roughy and gemfish.

Orange roughy are odd-looking, bug-eyed fish that form dense aggregations around deep-sea geological structures, such as undersea canyons and peaks. They also happen to be yummy, with deliciously flaky and tender white flesh. When large populations were discovered in the 1970s off the coasts of New Zealand, mainland Australia and Tasmania, they were so prolific some said that they could be caught by 'towing a chaff bag through the water'. The catches were so big that many boats, not equipped to handle such loads, simply burst their nets, and truckloads were dumped when numbers of the fish were too large to handle at the docks. By 1990, the worldwide catch had peaked at 90,000 tons, then steadily declined.

Gemfish followed the same formula: a staggering peak followed by an equally spectacular crash. A large commercial fishery was developed for gemfish off the New South Wales coast in the 1970s, with catches topping 5000 tons in 1980. Four years later, the haul was half that; nowadays the fishery has totally collapsed, with trawl catches currently at 100 tons for the 2022/23 season on the eastern fishing zone of Australia (and 340 tons in the west).

Today, in the early decades of the twenty-first century, fisheries are much more tightly managed and there's much greater scientific knowledge about the resilience of particular fish stocks. Many species, taken to the brink during decades of free-for-all fishing, are just starting to climb back.

The Catch

Commonwealth fisheries authorities – from catch sizes, fishing zones and seasons, down to the mesh size of nets.

The new catchwords weren't 'opportunity', 'potential' and 'expansion', but 'compliance', 'management' and 'risk assessment'.

To make up for the increased regulation, lower catches and squeezing margins, fisheries managers sensed the need for an industry bailout. In 2006, the Australian Government stumped up $200 million to buy out commercial fishing licences in an attempt to ensure that those who were left were able to make a profit that matched the investment of their time and labour. Five hundred and fifty licences were voluntarily surrendered, and those fishers either consolidated their existing businesses or left the industry altogether.

Since the introduction of an individual transferable quota system in 1992, where fishers were allocated limits on the catch numbers of particular species according to data on fish stocks, the number of commercial fishers has substantially declined, mostly through publicly funded buy-outs. From 1984 to 2000, commercial fishing licences in New South Wales alone fell from 3259 to 1686. Today, in 2023, that number is now about 1000.

If you couldn't ply the seas for fish any longer, what else could you do? Some moved into the next commercial fisheries frontier – aquaculture. If fish couldn't be caught sustainably, the fish farmers reasoned, why not simply grow them? And the aquaculture industry, particularly for Atlantic salmon, kingfish and southern bluefin tuna, has expanded significantly over the last decade.

Others shifted to tourism, transporting ecotourists to look for whales or dive with sharks from the old fishing ports of Eden, Port Lincoln and Albany. Or they became fishing guides and charter operators for cashed-up reccies looking for big game – the same reccies who'd fought commercial fishers for increased government management of fisheries, buy-outs and the creation of exclusion zones.

Many turned their backs on the fishing industry altogether. There was little point hanging around doing manual labour for next to nothing. For them, the sadness wasn't the fortune they lost – there usually wasn't any – but the life on the water they left behind.

The water has been receding steadily since the onset of the dry season, but the large billabong remains choked with rushes and weeds. Wading birds nervously stalk the water's edge, looking for small fish. They keep one eye out for the logs with eyes that emerge occasionally to survey the scene. Some of these crocs are bigger than the tinnies that have been lugged up to the Top End by countless fishos and their families.

They've been lured here (pun intended) with the promise of a trophy catch and an outdoors experience worthy of a social media feed.

CHAPTER 7

'A DAY FULL OF THUMPING FISH'
A RECCIE REVOLUTION

Technology was one of the game changers for recreational fishing in Australia following World War II. In the late 1950s, cheap, durable nylon lines became widely available, instantly replacing the heavy, unresponsive cotton and silk varieties that required constant maintenance. Inexpensive and flexible fibreglass rods quickly superseded the old split cane varieties. And mass-produced plastic and metal lures flooded the market, filling tackle shops with endless consumer choice.

The other catalyst was money. Australia enjoyed a long period of economic growth and high employment after the war, and the burgeoning middle class had more than ever to spend on travel and leisure. Car ownership became much more widespread and coincided with the increased provision of public amenities, such as campgrounds and public boat ramps.

Fishers and their families now had access to water beyond their immediate doorstep, and they had the time and money to get there. 'Now that the five-day week is with us, and man has more leisure hours, how will this free time be spent?' pondered one editorial in *The Australian Rod & Gun* in 1950. The answer was to be found in the great outdoors – including fishing.

The expansion of the rec-fishing scene also had an impact on the communities that came to depend on the tourism it generated. A growing range of cheap, accessible gear was available in tackle shops, holiday accommodation and tours were booked, and small fishing towns came to rely on the seasonal tourist trade – as did many of the communities around them. In New South Wales, money spent by recreational fishers supplemented incomes for many Aboriginal people, who organised fishing tours and packed worms in little plastic bags by the thousand to sell as bait.

Australian fishing and hunting magazines became a popular medium for the growing recreational market, with magazines such as *Angling & Gun Sport*, *Australian Shooters and Anglers News*, *Outdoors and Fishing: The Southern Hemisphere's Journal of the Great Outdoors*, *Anglers' Digest*, and, later, *The Australian Angler* and *Australian Sportfishing*. Even travel magazines, like *Walkabout*, included stories on fishing travel directed towards their growing, increasingly mobile readership. An antidote to the constraints of modern Australian suburbia lay in the holiday pursuit of fish, it seemed.

While those holidays were 'pre-eminently family time', renowned fishing writer Wal Hardy acknowledged in his 1955

article 'The Xmas Angle' in *Australian Outdoors & Fishing*, fishing
was in fact mostly for the blokes: 'lucky is the angler who can
take his family to a fishing resort to holiday by the seaside in
carefree spirit while he wears himself to the bone in pursuit
of fish'.

Reflecting that gendered division, the covers of fishing
and outdoors mags were generally graced by successful fishermen with their prized catches. Even the ads were geared
towards a distinctly male audience. And the tales that writers
spun echoed the drama and jocular bravado of early Australian fishing writing from the late nineteenth and early
twentieth centuries.

'The jaws of death are in the sea,' one story from *The
Australian Angler* in 1969 announced, rather melodramatically.
'They are the rocks that break bones. They are the shells that
strip flesh. They are the rips and the crushing power of the
ocean swells.' It was stirring stuff.

Two years later, Anthony James' story in *The Australian
Angler*, 'I Remember the Day', was decidedly more upbeat, but
no less adventurous. While 'I belong to that envious group of
Southerners who do most of their best "fishing" in the pages
of the national monthlies,' he admitted, a recent experience
catching tuna was something altogether different. Here was
'a day full of thumping fish with credentials that would frighten
the pants off a freshwater man'.

It wasn't just the Australian born who filled the caravan
parks and campgrounds springing up along the coast and
rivers further inland. Australia's post-war economic growth

was fuelled by a migration boom, in which Australia's population swelled by over one million new arrivals between 1945 and 1955. Like their Australian-born neighbours, many of those who ventured from Europe found themselves fishing at beachside camps or by the banks of the Swan, Murrumbidgee and Murray rivers on their weekends and summer holidays.

Camping and fishing was a popular and important way of taking in Australian culture and its landscape, and many migrants described their experiences fishing as part of their own Australian 'acclimatisation'. In turn, immigrants brought with them new fishing techniques and tastes. Now, when I launch my little kayak on the edge of Botany Bay it's not unusual to see old Greek Australian men tenderising octopus by flailing them across the concrete boat ramp, or Vietnamese Australians fishing at the mouth of the Cooks River.

If anything, that burgeoning, increasingly diverse post-war fishing enthusiasm has only expanded in recent decades. Retirees seasonally swell van parks and campsites across Australia's north, supplementing their superannuation with feeds of cherabin (freshwater prawns), mud crabs and bream.

Their children and grandchildren, meanwhile, populate an active cohort of weekend fishers and enthusiasts, who range from the occasional frequenter of jetties and bait shops to the most avid fisho who takes a rod or spear out daily.

City workers duck down to the water in between shifts, or have their lunchbreak overlooking the ocean, imagining the schools of kingfish or bonito that might be churning beneath the diving seabirds offshore. Those without the time find

WOMEN IN FISHING

In fishing magazines of the 1950s, women were present mostly as occasional cover girls. There was no shortage of trophy chicks with trophy fish. (Hardly surprising given the readership.) But women also fished back then, and there were several nods to the women fishers out there – a large, but generally silent, minority.

Stories such as 'Carol Took Me Tailor 'Ticing' and 'There's No Weaker Sex' (from *Anglers' Digest and Shooters' Monthly*) confirm the ongoing presence of fisherwomen, even if they don't hold back on their patronising attitudes. 'Goodness! We girls just don't know our own strength,' wrote Tess Travers in one of her early columns in *Outdoors and Fishing* in 1953. 'The age of male supremacy with the rod and reel is seriously being challenged.'

While women have always been part of the recreational fishing scene, both historically and today, their perspectives in fishing writing have been the exception rather than the rule. Despite this, the most recent published national survey of recreational fishing (2003), showed that women make up 30 per cent of rec-fishers. In many Indigenous communities, around 90 per cent of people fish regularly, including women.

Commercial fishing has also been a predominantly male scene in Australia. The labour involved in the industry – lengthy periods at sea, hours at dawn and dusk setting nets, and the hard physical labour – lent itself to a gendered division of work that still mostly remains. Yet women have been deeply involved in commercial fisheries, by mending nets, selling and buying catches and equipment, and processing fish on shore, as well as being involved in fisheries science. And by the late twentieth century, increased mechanisation has also meant women are more likely to make it out onto the boats to fish.

If the line-up of pink rods at Kmart is any indication, along with the proliferation of female-focused fishing programs and competitions, women and girls represent an important and growing consumer market today.

themselves chatting in online communities about promising sites, weather forecasts, productive lures and recent catches.

Taken together, these groups represent around five million recreational fishers in Australia in the early twenty-first century, and they have substantial consumer impact: they buy gear and tackle, they travel and book accommodation, they read magazines and guidebooks, they blog, they watch TV. *And* they fish.

So they notice when the catch starts to thin out. And when it does, they tend to lobby hard. Even by the 1960s, reccies expressed concern in fishing magazines that governments and fisheries needed to take more action to protect the recreational catch.

One correspondent to *Australian Sportfishing* in 1969 expressed his unease about the future of fishing in Australia. 'Angling, in all forms, has the greatest number of participants than any other sport in Australia . . . yet, in this country, little recognition is given to the fact that this sport has only a limited future, if conservation is not regarded as being equally important as participation.'

Slowly, but surely, the tide turned against commercial fisheries around Australia in favour of the reccies. In the quest for conservation, regulating commercial catches through licensing and quotas reduced catch limits and squeezed profit margins. It was an industry of diminishing, if more sustainable, returns.

The shift to increasing government support of recreational fishing was also economic and political. Millions of recreational fishers equate to billions of dollars injected into local economies as tourism and leisure.

But the raw economics were also tied up in political activism and lobbying. An unlikely alliance developed between conservation groups and recreational fishers, for example, who worked together to pressure governments to lock out commercial operators from key fishing areas.

Previously, the government-supported expansion of Australia's commercial fishing industry was done in the name of 'nation building' and 'progress'. But by the late twentieth century that national priority was waning, and favour had shifted to the image of the 'fisho'. Tension was inevitable.

In 1971, in response to reccies' demands, New South Wales State Fisheries announced that it would appoint a scientist to research the impact of commercial fishing on stocks in Botany Bay. A little further north, the Hawkesbury River was closed to commercial fishers on the weekends so a flotilla of tinnies could make their way up and down the estuary unimpeded. In 1980, the New South Wales Government even established a fisheries inquiry to investigate the emerging conflict between the recreational and commercial sectors.

By 2000, when Premier Bob Carr announced the introduction of recreational fishing licences to buy out the ninety commercial licences in Botany Bay, it was clear who was winning. In the eleven months following the introduction of rec-licences in New South Wales in 2001, 429,000 of the little laminated cards had been acquired, bringing in about nine million dollars of government revenue. A year later, the state government announced the establishment of twenty-nine fishing havens for reccies. Fishing as a primary industry, and in food production, was being overtaken by tourism and recreation.

The trend of closures and buy-outs of commercial fisheries happened around the country. In the Top End, river after river was closed to commercial barramundi fishing from the late 1980s. Then Darwin Harbour was too in 1998: barra safaris were worth more than brimming nets. 'The powerful voice of amateur fishing has captured the attention of governments, leaving professional fishermen gasping for oxygen,' penned journalist Paul Toohey in 2005. 'No government will stand between a man and his fish.'

But what about the impact of recreational fishing? While there had been sustained campaigns to reduce Australia's commercial take, little was known about rec-fishers – beyond the fact that there were an awful lot of them.

As it turns out, millions of fishers equate to millions of hooks being dropped into the water around Australia annually. According to one national survey, 'recreational fishers harvested approximately 136 million aquatic animals' in the twelve months leading up to May 2000.

A growing body of research into recreational fishing uncovered that those weekend flotillas were significantly impacting fish numbers, sometimes as much as the commercial industry. For example, the average size of speared eastern blue groper fell from 12 to 8 kilograms between 1952 and 1969, when it became protected from spear-fishing.

Meanwhile, the snapper catch data from old newspaper records suggest that today's hauls are roughly one-ninth the size of bags of fish caught in the late nineteenth and early twentieth centuries. This sort of research is painstakingly slow and involves combing through local reports and news items for old fishing stories, competition write-ups and catch records. Historical data are then compared to contemporary recreational data, including fishing surveys and competition results. Such studies reveal irrefutable evidence that even in largely recreational fisheries – such as snapper – fish numbers and sizes have steadily declined.

The seeds of those declining stock numbers had been embedded in the very fishing practices that assumed their inviolability: there was a time when fishers caught as much as they could. Given the apparent abundance of ocean life, there was little concern about conservation. Fish were simply a resource to be taken.

Nowadays, this all seems like ancient history. Watch a fishing show on TV and all you see is catch and release, with the odd snapper or kingfish kept for the plate. 'What is the point of killing fish just for the sake of it?' asks fishing icon Rex Hunt. 'All anglers must be conscious of the piscatorial environment and to kill fish you do not intend eating is environmental vandalism.'

By the time fish takes actually began to correspond with the dinner guests' appetites and catch-and-release fishing became the norm, however, the damage had already been done.

Several participants in an oral history of the Murray Basin gave accounts of 'an old mode of fishing best captured as take-all fishing', one of the authors, Jodi Frawley, later reflected.

'Testimony included stories of the trays of utility trucks loaded with fish, fish left in piles to rot on the riverbanks, fish tossed out at the end of a day's fishing and fish catches that could never equal the consumption habits of the individual fishers who caught them.'

Practices in my own family were no different, and great stories of fishing feats have been told around many a family dinner, filleting board or campfire – like the day my uncle and a mate caught forty-two tailor in an hour and a half back in 1976.

The pressure on stocks from rec-fishers couldn't last without some sort of noticeable effect, however. And, as numbers of fishers increased over the twentieth century, so did their impact.

Environmental repercussions were also felt beyond the catch itself. Great lengths of nylon line were discarded, polluting waterways with non-biodegradable plastic filament that wrapped around legs and fins or, even worse, were swallowed by unsuspecting fish and other marine animals. Metal and plastic lures were lost on snags. Waterways suffered bank erosion from high-powered boats, as well as pollution from campers and four-wheel drives. And hooks found their way into unintended bycatch, such as pelicans, cormorants and seals. Diminishing fish stocks also has consequences for the surrounding fisheries and food chains, so that when certain species get targeted (such as snapper or blue groper, for example) ecological systems can change.

What's more, the gear that enabled more fishers to get out on the water became much more efficient from the late twentieth century. Reccies now have fish finders and GPS devices on their boats, which pinpoint likely fishing spots and aggregations. They have access to lightweight tinnies with powerful engines, easily towed to locations near and far, as well as four-wheel drives that extend their range beyond the van parks and campgrounds of the 1950s. And they have new technologies that shift the advantage further away from their prey: chemically sharpened hooks, braided synthetic lines, geared reels and internet chat forums.

Governments responded to the growing body of research into recreational fishing in much the same way it had with the commercial industry: increased regulation, the introduction of fishing licences and education campaigns. In Queensland, the 1950s campaign to 'toss that tiddler' was superseded by new strategies a generation later, including the expansion of marine parks in an effort to change the behaviour of rec-fishers, encouraging more catch-and-release fishing. Meanwhile, fisheries officers actively police the harvesting of undersized catches, the use of illegal fishing gear, and fishing during closed seasons.

In 2004, the no-take areas of marine reserves in the Great Barrier Reef went from 5 to 33 per cent. Victorian fisheries similarly announced no-take marine protected areas. Marine reserves in New South Wales, prohibiting all forms of fishing, supplemented the commercial closures already enacted.

In Shark Bay, Western Australia, scientific monitoring in the late 1990s showed that the Eastern Gulf pink snapper fishery had effectively collapsed, since the spawning stock was down to less than 10 per cent of its estimated original population. Parts of the bay were completely closed to snapper fishing for several years, and when they reopened reccies had to enter a lottery to gain a seasonal licence. Even today, there are strict regulations for snapper catch and size limits.

Recent research revealed similarly precipitous stock data in South Australia. In response, the state government announced a total snapper closure in 2019 for recreational and commercial fishers in several fishing zones until at least 2026.

They have been bitter pills to swallow. The Victorian closures were met with howls of protest from anglers, despite the no-take zones amounting to roughly 6 per cent of state waters. Conservation closures elsewhere around Australia, such as on the Great Barrier Reef and in Sydney Harbour, elicited similar objections from fishers (and the industries they supported).

Recreational fishing agitators appealed to rights of access, arguing that they were the custodians of fisheries, since their own fishing futures hinged on good management. Rec-fishers also argued, with some merit, that they had been the original activists for fisheries management and reform. Now they were being disenfranchised by the very system they'd been calling for a generation earlier.

While some fishers applauded the shift towards greater conservation, others insisted that lockouts were too extreme. No-take zones might only be relatively small in terms of total water access, but these were often prime fishing locations readily accessible to the general public.

'Are we really going to get all worked up over this again?' asked 'Gumdrop', in an online fishing forum in 2014. 'It's only 20 per cent of the total area … Are we really so selfish we can't possibly forgo a small proportion of access for the sake of leaving part of [the] ecosystem in better condition and resilient to some of the other multitude of impacts it's exposed to?'

'Yes we are,' retorted 'Spiney'. 'The 20 per cent will be the most productive fishing areas so it will equate to much more. No use fishing in a desert.'

Fishers were being punished for the sins of their fathers and grandfathers, quite literally. And the wide-ranging powers that fisheries officers were given to enforce the new regulations have caused considerable resentment and unease among fishers across the board.

Governments and fisheries authorities were in an unenviable position, essentially forced to make contemporary laws in response to fishing practices a century old. And now they must manage the competing interests of the commercial and recreational industries, along with Traditional Owners seeking the restoration of sea rights.

In turn, the quest to balance fisheries management generated some tricky negotiations and policy-wrangling. The water is public, after all. But the issue of who should be able to access and fish that limited public resource, and how, generates considerable tension between diverse groups with competing interests.

Just how inviolable is the right to fish? The protection of fish populations sometimes closes off that public resource to the public, as the recreational fishing lobby rightly points out. Such measures, even when deemed necessary, generate significant criticism and backlash from different groups within the recreational fishing sector. Some reccies have been cut off from their special fishing place, perhaps after generations of fishing there.

Balancing the costs of lockouts to fishing communities with the ecological costs of doing nothing is an ongoing challenge for government departments and scientists around the country.

First Nations fishing rights prompts further difficult conversations. Fishing participation rates among Indigenous peoples sit as high as 92 per cent in some communities, where fishing is more a rite than a recreation – providing subsistence, connection to Country and sharing important cultural knowledge. What's more, the government regulation of sea rights in Australia, when sovereignty has never actually been ceded, is an irony not lost on many Indigenous fishers around the country.

Despite recognition of the cultural importance of fishing, access to traditional fisheries such as exceeding the bag-limit of abalone, or on-selling catches, has been heavily policed. And while Aboriginal and Torres Strait Islander peoples sustainably managed Australia's fisheries for thousands of years, any whiff of Indigenous 'special rights' generates resentment from many non-Indigenous rec-fishers.

Fisheries managers have a responsibility to protect vulnerable fish populations. Yet the prosecution of Aboriginal abalone 'poachers' for cultural fishing seems terribly unjust in some ways, given that the vulnerability of those stocks has been largely the result of non-Indigenous fishing practices in the first place. There are no easy answers.

Then there's still the question of the rights of commercial fisheries (big and small) to make a living producing and catching fish for general consumption. Increasing regulation has rightly curbed the excesses of unfettered extraction. The effects on fishing communities of diminishing numbers of licences and ever-tightening management, however, along with mounting costs and uncertain returns, has compounded the financial and psychological stress of countless fishing families and their communities.

Fishing remains a powerful, if at times conflicted, recreational activity in Australia today. During the COVID-19 pandemic, it became clear that access to our fishing spots went to the heart of many people's wellbeing and sense of self. Just being able to get outside was a huge relief for fishers and their families: the uncertainty of the pandemic could be forgotten out on the water and in the bush. It was a great reminder of the restorative power of being in nature.

For some, the importance of dropping a line extends to survival, literally, where fishing supplements the family economy with a few extra feeds here and there. In an era of rising costs of living, that economic imperative also needs to be accounted for.

Everyone wants to keep fishing, but our right to do that also presents critical challenges for the future management of fisheries: namely, are conservation and sustainability everybody's business? And if so, just how will they work?

CONCLUSION

'THE NEW NORMAL'
CAN WE KEEP FISHING?

It was an awful scene. At the tail end of a lengthy drought, during a hot, dry summer in 2019–20, the Baaka-Darling River stopped running. Its huge steep banks, once stepping-off points for a thriving river industry, now sloped down to little more than a chain of uninspiring ponds.

Down below, fish were gasping for air through the mud.

Enormous numbers of fish had died in previous black-water events during this drought. The most devastating had been during the previous summer, at Menindee Lakes in January 2019, when several hundred thousand fish were killed.

In a desperate attempt to prevent a repeat catastrophe, local landowners, volunteers and fisheries officers tried to trap and relocate as many fish as possible – especially surviving big breeders.

Like Aboriginal fishers a thousand years earlier, they waded through the water with long hand-held nets, splashing the surface to drive fish into the mesh. But this wasn't a casual afternoon catching a feed with family. And the fishery wasn't anything like the one Sturt had encountered on his wanderings through inland New South Wales nearly 200 years previously.

There had always been droughts here. But the sight of enormous Murray cod cradled like babies before being transported to more secure waterholes was an image seared into people's minds. How could this happen?

Meanwhile, further east, enormous fires sparked in the tinder-dry bush and hurtled towards coastal towns. From Queensland right around to South Australia, trees were scorched like matchsticks. It's estimated that three billion native animals were impacted that summer.

Footage of holiday makers sheltering from flames in their tinnies out on the water, or hunkering together on the beaches as the fires roared closer, was another image that won't be readily forgotten. Fishing felt like a distant memory. Was this the new normal? Spending summer hiding from firestorms?

Oceans also seemed increasingly vulnerable at this moment. In Queensland, the United Nations Educational, Scientific and Cultural Organization (UNESCO) indicated it would classify the Great Barrier Reef as officially 'in danger', given its precarious exposure to climate change.

Increasing and intensifying coral bleaching, as well as ongoing degradation caused by agricultural run-off, has damaged the biodiversity of that immense ecological system to an extent that once seemed unimaginable. Reefs, once the site of outrageous and lurid coral gardens, became grey and brittle after suffering from repeated bleaching events. Elsewhere around the Pacific, thousands of square kilometres of dead and dying coral reefs are an indication of where we might end up. Changing water temperatures and acidification caused by climate change add further stresses to marine environments already under pressure from fishing.

This isn't the first time fishers and fisheries managers have been stopped in their tracks by rapid environmental change in Australia.

As we've seen throughout this book, rapacious and intensive extraction during the nineteenth and twentieth centuries brought key fisheries to the brink. In the 1800s, local stocks were quickly exploited by rapidly growing colonies. In particular, the demand for lime mortar created an insatiable appetite for oysters, prompting a rolling exploration for new beds to dredge – until there were none left.

Across southern Australia, over 90 per cent of native oyster reefs have disappeared. In Port Phillip Bay alone, while oysters and blue mussels can still be found, they are a tiny fraction of the shellfish reef systems that were once endemic. Now they're classified as 'functionally extinct'.

Over the course of the twentieth century, industrial fishing practices triggered the collapse of several other fisheries: tiger flathead, bluefin tuna, orange roughy, gemfish. Each species represents a story of excited 'exploration', 'discovery' and 'exploitation' – not unlike those grand progress narratives of colonial Australia. Like Burke, Wills and Leichhardt, however, these 'pioneering stories' often ended in tragedy.

Boom was mostly followed by bust.

Other pressures also adversely impacted fish populations. The dumping of rubbish and sewage into the ocean was long considered practical and resourceful. As several Sydney councils offloaded their waste by barge at sea, including domestic and abattoir waste, dead kittens, carcasses and rotten fruit, high faecal coliform levels were endemic at Sydney's beaches during the twentieth century. Add in the nitrogenous run-off from fertilisers, industrial pollution and dredging, and you have a series of major stressors on fish habitat.

Industrialisation made our nation incredibly wealthy, and generations of Australians worked hard to create that pros- perity and security. But growth has come at the expense of the natural world.

The environmental historian Tom Griffiths describes what happened to Australia in modern times as a 'profound rupture' in its history and ecology. Low-population, low-impact, largely sustainable systems of Indigenous land and water manage- ment that functioned for upwards of sixty thousand years were rapidly replaced with a model of constant, extractive growth.

Fisheries management eventually responded to the alarming decline in stocks, introducing wide-ranging legislation across recreational and commercial sectors. But it hasn't been easy. Part of the problem has been the challenge of mapping just what has been lost. The ecological cleavage of moderni- sation resulted in a form of 'generational amnesia', as marine ecologists Heidi Alleway and Sean Connell have argued, where actual knowledge of what our fisheries 'used to be like' has incrementally disappeared.

It's a classic case of what marine biologist Daniel Pauly famously called 'shifting baseline syndrome'. The concept describes how generations can only remember what fisheries were like at the beginning of their own lifetimes, so that, bit by bit, the baseline of that ecosystem changes over time. This changing reference point has produced what environmental historians Andrea Gaynor and Joy McCann describe as a 'progressively poorer natural world', where an ever-lower bar is set as the 'new normal'.

If our natural history is increasingly harder to remember, the possibility of getting back to a version of sustainability presents huge challenges.

How do we deal with 'trawler trash' in the prawn and trawl industries that has an estimated bycatch discard rate of around 40 per cent? The introduction of bycatch reduction devices from the late 1990s halved this (from an original figure closer to 80 or 90 per cent). Yet the tally of discards over a century still amounts to millions of tonnes of junked fish, with mixed survival rates. And unwanted or undersized species are still thrown overboard after every haul of a fishing net.

Then there's the question of monitoring recreational fishing, which uses patchy and sporadic data to understand and regulate its impact. Estimating recreational catches is extremely difficult, relying on local surveys, commercial catch numbers and extrapolation. Those weekend catches of bream or squid by families right around the country are impossible to aggregate accurately. But they all add up.

Although taking much-needed pressure off the hunting of wild stocks, certain forms of aquaculture can also be fraught. While farming filter feeders such as oysters and mussels can actually improve water quality, intensive fin-fish aquaculture can damage vulnerable ecosystems.

When giant pens corral fish in tight proximity, the threat of disease is always close and fish waste can pollute delicate waterways if not managed correctly. The fish-feed required to farm intensively also puts pressure on the seafood chain. Fish farming will inevitably be part of the solution for sustainable fisheries, but just how that industry is managed into the future remains a work in progress.

Australians' love of fishing constitutes a bit of a paradox. The joy of being outdoors, of fishing by ourselves or with our families can't be measured. Neither can the lives and livelihoods of those who fish for a living. But fish stocks need to be.

Our right to fish continues to be complicated by emerging research. So much is still unknown about Australia's fisheries. New, sometimes alarming, data comes to light every year.

In 2022, sand flathead populations were deemed to be on the verge of collapse in Tasmania after generations of being a favoured recreational catch. We now know the actual time it takes for yellowtail kingfish to reach sexual maturity, which has prompted changes to the catch and size limits for this popular table fish. And the latest information about mulloway stocks in New South Wales reveals they're now well under 20 per cent of virgin biomass (and that figure is possibly as low as 10 per cent).

In Commonwealth waters, the 2022 report from the Australian Bureau of Agricultural and Resource Economics and Sciences (ABARES) revealed that in 2021 sixty-nine stocks 'were classified as not overfished', thirteen 'were classified as overfished' and nineteen 'were classified as uncertain with regard to biomass status'. There isn't enough data to determine their population, even though we've had more than a century of fisheries research and management.

And, despite the increasing monitoring and control of Australian waters, we're still implicated in the global market and its history. Australian fisheries are some of the most regulated in the world, but we buy the majority of our seafood from elsewhere.

Around 60 to 70 per cent of fish consumed in Australia comes from overseas. Prawn farms in Vietnam, tuna poling in Alaska, longlining in the Pacific and cod fisheries in the North Sea are everybody's business, especially when you consider that the number of fish stocks globally classified as seriously overfished was nearly 50 per cent by 2000. According to the Food and Agriculture Organization of the United Nations (FAO) in 2022, the fraction of fishery stocks within biologically sustainable levels decreased from 90 per cent in 1974 to 64.6 per cent in 2019. At the same time, the percentage of stocks fished at biologically unsustainable levels has been increasing since the late 1970s, from 10 per cent in 1974 to 35.4 per cent in 2019.

Drought, floods, water rights, climate change, fisheries science, regulating international practice: each presents a huge challenge in its own right. Taken together, the task of fisheries management might seem insurmountable.

Yet those challenges of fisheries management have also forged some curious and inspiring alliances between conservation groups and recreational fishing and hunting groups, who have agitated for marine protected areas. Similar coalitions have campaigned for increased freshwater flows in inland waterways, along with further regulation of water extraction, floodplain harvesting and irrigation. At the same time, local volunteer land-care groups, fisheries scientists and recreational fishing clubs have banded together in an impressive network of habitat restoration projects in an attempt to secure healthy waterways and fish populations.

While that image of a volunteer cradling a giant Murray cod felt like the manifestation of some terrifying endpoint when rivers in New South Wales stopped running during the 2019–20 drought, it also demonstrated our desperation to keep fishing and our commitment to make that possible.

Right around the country, in fresh water and salt, there is a growing effort to ensure we can keep fishing into the future. Along roads and tracks, causeways are being slowly replaced with fish-friendly drainage so fish and eels can move across water catchments during and after rain events. Fishways are being installed next to weirs, allowing the seasonal migration of native species.

Rivers that were dynamited and dredged to allow easier boat access, or tidal flushing, are being re-snagged. Enormous root balls are carefully craned onto new underwater beds. In time, fish will also find their way there, attracted to the protective, tuberous web that makes for ideal habitat.

Shellfish reefs that were dredged into oblivion are being reseeded with layers of limestone and shells, creating an ideal environment for rebuilding. Juvenile oysters and mussels, grown in fish hatcheries, are gently deposited on top to grow into new reef systems.

Sea grasses and kelp are being replanted at key sites in an attempt to restore the biodiversity essential for fish habitat and breeding. Coral is being harvested and studied in laboratories and onsite to assess which species are likely to be most resilient to climate change.

This is no solo effort, but disparate pieces of a complex fishing puzzle that requires collaboration and connection – between landowners and fisheries scientists, governments and local communities, conservationists and fishing groups, lobbyists and business owners. It's creating a new wave of citizen science and fostering leagues of volunteers, while also overcoming and complicating long-held political divisions.

And while these connections represent important new allegiances and relationships, they also depend on the recognition of older knowledges, like Indigenous management of Country. The increasing, if belated, acknowledgement of Indigenous understandings of Australia's fisheries and waterways presents profound opportunities to think about sustainability and intergenerational responsibility, as well as the rights of Country itself.

The Catch

Fishing knowledge has always been handed down. The choicest spots, the best hole to find crays, the safest rock to stand on when the swell's up, or the most productive reef (a closely guarded family secret!). This current moment of habitat restoration and fisheries sustainability includes the realisation that passing on our favourite pastime can't be taken for granted.

Future generations depend on it.

IMAGE CREDITS

p. xii   Unknown, *Fishing – Murrumbidgee, 1949*, Mitchell Library, State Library of New South Wales, ON 388/Box 073/Item 211.

p. 8   Joseph Banks, *Banks Papers – Series 36a: Charts and illustrations, ca 1790s*, '5. Watercolour Illustration of a Group of Aborigines Fishing, ca 1790s – Attributed to Philip Gidley King', 1803, Mitchell Library, State Library of New South Wales, SAFE/Banks Papers/Series 36a (Safe 1/457).

p. 28   Thomas Skottowe, *Select Specimens*, '46. Groper (no.8); Parrot Fish (no.9); Unicorn Fish or Leather Jacket (no.10); Salmon (no.11)', 1813, Mitchell Library, State Library of New South Wales, SAFE/PXA 555.

p. 44   Unknown, *Mending the Nets*, State Library of Western Australia, b3048982_1.

p. 62   Sam Hood, *Fly Fishing in the Stream*, 1930s, State Library of New South Wales, Home and Away – 7167.

p. 76   Harold Cazneaux, *Fishing Off Rocks*, 1904, National Library of Australia, nla.obj-140207732.

p. 94   Ern McQuillan, *Tuna Fishing at Eden, New South Wales*, 1960, National Library of Australia, nla.obj-137011608.

p. 114   Jim Harnwell, *Creek*, 2006.

p. 132   Anna Clark, *Fishing from the Point*, Wapengo, 2019.

Credits for all full-colour images are listed in the order in which they appear:

Joseph Lycett, *Aboriginal Australians Spearing Fish and Diving for Shellfish, New South Wales*, c. 1817, National Library of Australia, nla.obj-138500727.

Glass plate negative, full plate, 'Aboriginal fisheries, Darling River', 1880–1923, photography by unattributed studio, Tyrrell Collection, Powerhouse collection. Gift of Australian Consolidated Press under the Taxation Incentives for the Arts Scheme, 1985.

M. Dubourg, *Fishing No. 1*, 1813, National Library of Australia, nla.obj-135898881.

Joseph Lycett, *Aboriginal Australians Night Fishing by Fire Torches, New South Wales*, c. 1817, National Library of Australia, nla.obj-138499378.

Mickey of Ulladalla, *Fishing Activities of Aboriginal Australian People and Settlers Near Ulladulla, New South Wales, Approximately 1885*, c. 1880–1890, National Library of Australia, nla.obj-135516869.

Joseph Swabey Tetley, *Natives of New South Wales*, '12. Aboriginal Woman in a Canoe Fishing With a Line', c. 1805, Mitchell Library, State Library of New South Wales, PXB 513.

Anna Clark. *Kakadu Rock Face*, 2008.

Unknown, *Macquarie Collector's Chest*, 'An Array of Fish on the Top Lid', c. 1818, Mitchell Library, State Library of New South Wales, XR 69, MLMSS 8628.

Unknown, *Fish Market at Woolloomooloo, N.S.W.*, Melbourne: Ebenezer and David Syme, 1875, State Library of Victoria, PCINF IAN 01-12-75 P.196.

Unknown, *Chinese Drying Fresh Fish in the Sun – Tamworth, NSW*, 1880–1940, Mitchell Library, State Library of New South Wales, At Work and Play – 01328.

Dennis Brabazon, *A Ninety-seven Pound Murray Cod, Caught by a Professional Fisherman Near Collendina Station in the Corowa District, New South Wales*, 1924, National Library of Australia, nla.obj-141679505.

E. W. (Edward William) Searle, *Three Men and Three Women Fishing from a Log in the Middle of a River, Australia*, between 1890 and 1910, National Library of Australia, nla.obj-141932646.

Unknown, *Trout Fishing at Eildon Weir – Pix Series*, c. 1950, Mitchell Library, State Library of New South Wales, ON 388/Box 056/Item 129.

Image credits

J. Bagnell, *Spear Fishing Long Reef, 4 April 1948*, 1948, Mitchell Library, State Library of New South Wales, ON 388/Box 053/Item 192.

Gibbs, Shallard & Co., *Fishing, A Sketch in Mossman's Bay, Port Jackson*, October 1871, National Library of Australia, nla.obj-133181941.

Sydney Mail (NSW: 1912–1938), 29 October 1919, p. 1, National Library of Australia, ISSN: 22026045.

Unknown, *Approach to Cave Dwellers House Near Kernell [i.e. Kurnell], New South Wales*, 1930s, National Library of Australia, nla.obj-150885108.

Unknown, *Unemployed Men Fishing with Homemade Rods During the Great Depression*, c. 1930, National Library of Australia, nla.obj-141685523.

Jeff Carter, *Salmon Netting, Kendall's Beach, Kiama, New South Wales*, 1967, National Library of Australia, nla.obj-137334266.

Ruth Maddison and Julie Fourter, *Guy Robert on Osprey IV Climbing Mound of Orange Roughy, A Deep Sea Fish*, Portland, Victoria, 1988, National Library of Australia, nla.obj-150931639.

Jim Harnwell, *Trout*, 2010.

Jim Harnwell, *Whiting*, c. 2000.

Jim Harnwell, *Marlin*, 2016.

Darren Clark, *Fishing in the Still Waters of an East Kimberley River*, 2018, Darren Clark collection of photographs State Library of Western Australia BA2840/528.

NSW Department of Primary Industries, *Releasing Juvenile Mulloway in the Georges River*, 2023.

OzFish Unlimited, *Matt Hansen Murray Cod Macquarie River Fish Rescue*, 2019.

Jim Harnwell, *Coral Trout*, 2022.

ENDNOTES

Introduction

p. 4–5 Gary W. Henry and Jeremy M. Lyle, *The National Recreational and Indigenous Fishing Survey*, Canberra: Australian Government Department of Agriculture, Fisheries and Forestry, 2003, p.133.

p. 5 Fisheries Research and Development Corporation, 'National Recreational Fishing Survey: update', 2022: frdc.com.au/about-recreational-fishing/nrfs (accessed 31 March 2023); Shane P. Griffiths, Joanne Bryant, Henry F. Raymond and Peter A. Newcombe, 'Quantifying Subjective Human Dimensions of Recreational Fishing: Does Good Health Come to Those Who Bait?', *Fish and Fisheries*, vol. 18, no. 1, 2017, pp. 171–84; Elizabeth Baker, 'Recreational Fishers in Australia: A Social Snapshot', Ballina, NSW: OzFish Unlimited, 2017: ozfish.org.au/wp-content/uploads/2017/05/Recreational-Fishers-in-Australia-a-social-snapshot-sml.pdf (accessed 24 April 2023); Caitlin Fitzsimmons, '"If It All Goes Wrong, I'd Rather Be on the Water": Covid-19 Sparks Boating Boom', *Sydney Morning Herald*, 17 January 2021.

p. 5 Robert Hughes, *A Jerk on One End: Reflections of a Mediocre Fisherman*, London: Harvill Press, 1999, pp. 5, 11.

p. 6 Jodi Frawley, 'Kissing fish: Rex Hunt, Popular Culture, Sustainability and Fishing Practices', *Journal of Australian Studies*, vol. 39, no. 3, 2015, p. 316.

Chapter 1

p. 9   John Turnbull, *A Voyage Round the World In the Years 1800, 1801, 1802, 1803, and 1804, in Which the Author Visited the Principal Islands in the Pacific Ocean and the English Settlements of Port Jackson and Norfolk Island* (vol. 1), London: Richard Phillips, 1805, pp. 84–5; Watkin Tench, *A Complete Account of the Settlement at Port Jackson*, Sydney: University of Sydney Library, 1998.

p. 11   Australian Museum, 'Aboriginal People of Coastal Sydney: Place Names Chart': australianmuseum.net.au/place-names-chart (accessed 13 April 2023).

p. 11   For *malgun*, see: Grace Karskens, *The Colony: A History of Early Sydney*, Crows Nest, NSW: Allen & Unwin, 2009, p. 39; Val Attenbrow, *Sydney's Aboriginal Past*, Sydney: UNSW Press, 2010, p. 64; Alex Roberts, *Aboriginal Women's Fishing in New South Wales: A Thematic History*, Sydney: Department of Environment, Climate Change and Water NSW, 2010, pp. 9–10; Martin Thomas (ed.), *Culture in Translation: The Anthropological Legacy of R. H. Mathews*, Canberra: ANU Press, 2007, pp. 53–4; G. Paterson, *The History of New South Wales: From its First Discovery to the Present Time*, Newcastle-upon-Tyne: MacKenzie and Dent, 1811, p. 104; David Collins, *An Account of the English Colony in New South Wales With Remarks on the Dispositions, Customs, Manners, &c., of the Native Inhabitants of that Country. To which are Added, Some Particulars of New Zealand*, London: T. Cadell, jun. and W. Davies, 1798, pp. 358–9.

p. 12   Making fishing line: Beryl Cruse, Liddy Stewart and Sue Norman, *Mutton Fish*, Canberra: Aboriginal Studies Press, 2005, p. 4; Roberts, *Aboriginal Women's Fishing in New South Wales*, p. 23; J. G. Pepperell, 'The Good Old Days? Historical Insights into Coastal NSW Fish Populations and their Fisheries', Sydney: The NSW Recreational Fishing Trusts Expenditure Committee, N.D, p. 29.

p. 12   Tench, *A Complete Account of the Settlement at Port Jackson*, p. 193.

p. 13   In Queensland, some fishers on Keppel Island were reported to spear enormous groper after berleying the water with oysters: Noel Haysom, *Trawlers, Trollers and Trepangers: The Story of the Queensland Commercial Fishing Industry pre-1988*, Brisbane: QLD Department of Primary Industries, 2001, p. 1. In Western Australia, ground shellfish were scattered into the water to attract fish for spearing: Andrea

Endnotes

Gaynor, 'Shifting Baselines or Shifting Currents? An Environmental History of Fish and Fishing in the South-west Capes Region of Western Australia', in J. Christensen and M. Tull (eds), *Historical Perspectives of Fisheries Exploitation in the Indo-Pacific*, New York: Springer, 2006, p. 235.

p. 13   Roberts, *Aboriginal Women's Fishing in New South Wales*, pp. 18–9; Karskens, *The Colony*, p. 39; T. C. Roughley, *Fish and Fisheries of Australia*, Sydney: Angus & Robertson, 1951, pp. 325–6; Paterson, *The History of New South Wales*, pp. 104–5.

p. 13   David Collins, *An Account of the English Colony in New South Wales*, pp. 592–3.

p. 13   Louis de Freycinet, *Voyage autour du monde entrepris par ordre du Roi . . . exécuté sur les corvettes de S. M. l'Uranie et la Physicienne, pendant les années 1817, 1818, 1819 et 1820, historique, tome deuxième – deuxième partie*, Paris: Chez Pillet Aîné, 1839, p. 775. See also the Austral harmony site of music historians: Graeme Skinner and Jim Wafer, 'A Checklist of Colonial Era Musical Transcriptions of Australian Indigenous Songs': sydney.edu.au/paradisec/australharmony/checklist-indigenous-music-1.php#005-2 (accessed 15 December 2022).

p. 14   John Heaviside Clark, *Field Sports &c. &c. of the Native Inhabitants of New South Wales: With Ten Plates by the Author*, London: Edward Orme, 1813, p. 30.

p. 14   Roughley, *Fish and Fisheries of Australia*, p. 327.

p. 18   R. H. Mathews, 'The Aboriginal Fisheries at Brewarrina', *Journal and Proceedings of the Royal Society of New South Wales*, vol. 37, 1903, p. 150; Bruce Pascoe, *Dark Emu: Black Seeds – Agriculture or Accident?*, Broome, WA: Magabala Books, 2014, pp. 55–8.

p. 18   Sarah Martin, Hubert Chanson, Badger Bates, Duncan Keenan-Jones and Michael C. Westaway, 'Indigenous Fish Traps and Fish Weirs on the Darling (Baaka) River, South-eastern Australia, and their Influence on the Ecology and Morphology of the River and Floodplains', *Archaeology in Oceania*, 2022, pp. 1–24.

p. 18   Peter Dargin, *Aboriginal Fisheries of the Darling–Barwon Rivers*, Brewarrina, NSW: Brewarrina Historical Society, 1976, p. 21.

p. 19   Ian McNiven, Joe Crouch, Thomas Richards, Kale Sniderman, Nic Dolby and Gunditj Mirring, 'Phased Redevelopment of an

Ancient Gunditjmara Fish Trap over the Past 800 Years: Muldoons Trap Complex, Lake Condah, Southwestern Victoria', *Australian Archaeology*, vol. 81, no. 1, 2015, pp. 44–58.

p. 19   John William Wills (ed.), *A Successful Exploration through the Interior of Australia: From Melbourne to the Gulf of Carpentaria / from the Journals and Letters of William John Wills. Edited by His Father, William Wills*, London: Richard Bentley, 1863, p. 195.

p. 20   Kim Barber and Hilary Rumley, 'Gunanurang: (Kununurra) Big River Aboriginal Cultural Values of the Ord River and Wetlands', Perth: The Water and Rivers Commission, WA, 2003, p. 19.

p. 20   Arthur Phillip, *The Voyage of Governor Phillip to Botany Bay: With an Account of the Establishment of the Colonies of Port Jackson and Norfolk Island*, Sydney: University of Sydney Library, 2003, p. 88; Dargin, *Aboriginal Fisheries of the Darling–Barwon Rivers*, p. 22; Mary Gilmore, *Old Days – Old Ways*, Sydney: Angus and Robertson, 1963, ch. 27; Roughley, *Fish and Fisheries of Australia*, p. 318.

p. 20   Dargin, *Aboriginal Fisheries of the Darling–Barwon Rivers*, p. 25.

p. 21   ibid., pp. 23–5; Charles Sturt, *Two Expeditions into the Interior of Southern Australia During the Years 1828, 1829, 1830, 1831: With Observations on the Soil, Climate, and General Resources of the Colony of New South Wales*, Sydney: University of Sydney Library, 2001.

pp. 21–2 Paterson, *The History of New South Wales*, p. 105; Cruse, *Mutton Fish*, p. 4; Jodi Frawley, Scott Nichols, Heather Goodall and Liz Baker, *Talking Fish: Making Connections with the Rivers of the Murray Darling Basin*, Canberra: Murray Darling Basin Authority, 2012; 'Aboriginal Women's Heritage: Port Stephens', Sydney: Department of Environment and Conservation NSW, 2004; 'Aboriginal People Living and Working on the NSW Coast: A Historical Review', Sydney: Office of Environment and Heritage NSW, 2012; Pascoe, *Dark Emu*, ch. 2.

p. 22   Gilmore, *Old Days – Old Ways*, p. 208; Roughley, *Fish and Fisheries of Australia*, p. 319.

p. 22   Barber and Rumley, 'Gunanurang', p. 19.

p. 22   Lindsay Thompson, *History of the Fisheries of New South Wales: With a Sketch of the Laws by which They Have Been Regulated*, Sydney: Government Printer, 1893, p. 95.

Endnotes

p. 23   Dargin, *Aboriginal Fisheries of the Darling–Barwon Rivers*, p. 22; Alex Roberts, *Aboriginal Women's Fishing in New South Wales: A Thematic History*, Sydney: Department of Environment, Climate Change and Water NSW, 2010, p. 20.

p. 23   Watkin Tench, *A Complete Account of the Settlement at Port Jackson*, Sydney, University of Sydney Library, 1998 [first published 1793], p. 176; Roberts, *Aboriginal Women's Fishing in New South Wales*, p. 15.

p. 23   Roberts, *Aboriginal Women's Fishing in New South Wales*, p. 19.

p. 23   Frances Bodkin, *D'harawal Seasons and Climate Cycles*, Sydney: F. Bodkin and L. Robertson, 2008, pp. 25, 33, 59. Frances Bodkin's compilation of D'harawal stories and knowledge demonstrates the way in which D'harawal people used seasonal indicators to guide their fishing practices. In contrast, the flowering of *Burringoa* (*Eucalyptus tereticornis*), which signifies the coming of cold weather, indicates 'that it is a time when the people are not permitted to eat shellfish such as prawns, crabs, yabbies, mussels, pipis, lobsters or periwinkles'. The buds of the waratah and first appearances of flying foxes in the skies indicate the lifting of these restrictions, and 'feasting on the beaches and river banks occurs'.

p. 24   Bob Dunn, *Angling in Australia: Its History and Writings*, Balmain, NSW: David Ell Press, 1991, p. 16.

p. 24   Ian McNiven, 'Saltwater People: Spiritscapes, Maritime Rituals and the Archaeology of Australian Indigenous Seascapes', *World Archaeology*, vol. 35, no. 3, 2004, pp. 329–49.

p. 25   Martin et al., 'Indigenous Fish Traps and Fish Weirs on the Darling (Baaka) River', pp. 1–24; Ian Hoskins, *Coast*, Sydney: NewSouth Publishing, 2013, p. 161; Danielle Clode, *Killers in Eden: The True Story of Killer Whales and their Remarkable Partnership with the Whalers of Twofold Bay*, Crows Nest, NSW: Allen & Unwin, 2002.

p. 25   Attenbrow, *Sydney's Aboriginal Past*, p. 64.

p. 25   William Bradley, *Journal titled 'A Voyage to New South Wales', December 1786 – May 1792*, Mitchell Library, State Library of New South Wales, 1802, p. 132: acms.sl.nsw.gov.au/_transcript/2015/D02131/a138.html (accessed 13 April 2023); Roberts, *Aboriginal Women's Fishing in New South Wales*, p. 12; Attenbrow, *Sydney's Aboriginal Past*, p. 64.

p. 25 Eric A. Colhoun and Adrian Piper, 'Stone Fish Traps at Cooks Corner, Freycinet Peninsula, Eastern Tasmania', *Australian Archaeology*, vol. 14, 1982, pp. 115–8; Jim Stockton, 'Stone Wall Fish Traps in Tasmania', *Australian Archaeology*, vol. 14, 1982, pp. 107–14; Rebe Taylor, 'The Polemics of Eating Fish in Tasmania: the Historical Evidence Revisited', *Aboriginal History*, vol. 32, 2007, pp. 1–26; Ian Walters, 'Prehistoric Fisheries in Australia: A Long and Diverse Pedigree', *Australian Fisheries*, vol. 46, no. 3, 1987, pp. 21–4; Billy Griffiths, *Deep Time Dreaming: Uncovering Ancient Australia*, Carlton, Vic: Black Inc, 2018, pp. 73–6; Rhys Jones, 'The Tasmanian Paradox', in R. V. S. Wright (ed.), *Stone Tools as Cultural Markers: Change, Evolution and Complexity*, Canberra: Australian Institute of Aboriginal Studies, 1977, pp. 189–204; Josephine Flood, *The Original Australians: The Story of the Aboriginal People*, Sydney: Allen & Unwin, 2019, pp. 87–9; Peter Hiscock, *Archaeology of Ancient Australia*, London & New York: Routledge, 2008, pp. 133–9.

Chapter 2

p. 29 Joseph Hooker (ed.), *Journal of the Right Hon. Sir Joseph Banks . . . During Captain Cook's First Voyage in* H.M.S. Endeavour *in 1768–71 to Terra del Fuego, Otahite, New Zealand, Australia, the Dutch East Indies, etc.*, London: Macmillan & Co., Ltd, 1896, p. 263.

p. 30 Hooker (ed.), *Journal of the Right Hon. Sir Joseph Banks*, p. 264.

p. 31 James Cook entry for 30 April 1770, *Journal of H.M.S. Endeavour*, 1768–1771, MS 1, National Library of Australia.

p. 32 Hooker (ed.), *Journal of the Right Hon. Sir Joseph Banks*, p. 269; Val Attenbrow, *Sydney's Aboriginal Past*, Sydney: UNSW Press, 2010, p. 64.

p. 32 Hooker (ed.), *Journal of the Right Hon. Sir Joseph Banks*, p. 269.

p. 32 Regina Ganter, 'Muslim Australians: The Deep Histories of Contact', *Journal of Australian Studies*, vol. 32, no. 4, 2008, pp. 482–3; Campbell Macknight, '"The view from Marege": Australian Knowledge of Makassar and the Impact of the Trepang Industry Across Two Centuries', *Aboriginal History*, vol. 35, 2011, pp. 127–38; Noel Haysom, *Trawlers, Trollers and Trepangers: The Story of the Queensland Commercial Fishing Industry pre-1988*, Brisbane: QLD Department of Primary Industries, 2001, pp. 18–9.

Endnotes

p. 33   Hooker (ed.), *Journal of the Right Hon. Sir Joseph Banks*, pp. 269–79.

p. 33   University of Wollongong, 'First Fleet Database': firstfleet.uow. edu.au/index.html (accessed 13 April 2023); First Fleet Fellowship Victoria Inc., 'List of Livestock and Provisions': firstfleetfellowship. org.au/library/first-fleetlist-livestock-provisions-plants-seeds/ (accessed 13 April 2023).

p. 36   Crew on the First Fleet did fish on the way over, with reported catches of bonito: John White, *Journal of a Voyage to New South Wales*, London: Debrett, 1790.

p. 36   Ralph Clark, *The Journal and Letters of Lt Ralph Clark 1787 – 1792*, Sydney: University of Sydney Library, 1981; George B. F. S. Worgan, *Journal of a First Fleet Surgeon*, Sydney: University of Sydney Library, 2003; J. G. Pepperell, 'The Good Old Days? Historical Insights into Coastal NSW Fish Populations and their Fisheries', Sydney, The NSW Recreational Fishing Trusts Expenditure Committee, N.D., pp. 18–20.

p. 36   John C. Dann (ed.), *The Nagle Journal: A Diary of the Life of Jacob Nagle, Sailor, from the Year 1775 to 1841*, New York: Weidenfeld & Nicolson, c. 1988, p. 94; Bob Dunn, *Angling in Australia: Its History and Writings*, Balmain, NSW: David Ell Press, 1991, p. 60.

pp. 36–7 David Collins, *An Account of the English Colony in New South Wales With Remarks on the Dispositions, Customs, Manners, &c., of the Native Inhabitants of that Country. To which are Added, Some Particulars of New Zealand*, London: T. Cadell, jun. and W. Davies, 1798, p. 74.

p. 37   Arthur Phillip, *The Voyage of Governor Phillip to Botany Bay: With an Account of the Establishment of the Colonies of Port Jackson and Norfolk Island*, Sydney: University of Sydney Library, 2003, p. 75.

p. 37   Collins, *An Account of the English Colony of New South Wales*, p. 92.

p. 38   E. W. Dunlop, 'John Joseph Oxley', *Australian Dictionary of Biography*: adb.anu.edu.au/biography/oxley-john-joseph-2530 (accessed 13 April 2023).

p. 38   John Oxley, *Journals of Two Expeditions into the Interior of New South Wales Undertaken by Order of the British Government in the Years 1817–18*, Sydney: University of Sydney Library, 2002, 6 May 1820. See also: Stuart Rowland, 'Overview of the History, Fishery, Biology and Aquaculture of Murray Cod (Maccullochella peelii peelii)', Management of

Murray Cod in the Murray–Darling Basin Workshop, 3–4 June 2004, Canberra, Murray–Darling Basin Commission.

p. 39   Ludwig Leichhardt, *Journal of an Overland Expedition in Australia, from Moreton Bay to Port Essington, a Distance of Upwards of 3000 Miles, During the Years 1844–1845*, London: T. & W. Boone, 1847, p. 105.

pp. 39–40 William John Wills (ed.), *A Successful Exploration through the Interior of Australia: From Melbourne to the Gulf of Carpentaria / from the Journals and Letters of William John Wills. Edited by His Father, William Wills*, London: Richard Bentley, 1863, p. 184; Michael Cathcart, *Starvation in a Land of Plenty*, Canberra: NLA Publishing, 2013; Sarah Murgatroyd, *The Dig Tree: The Story of Burke and Wills*, Melbourne: Text Publishing, 2012.

p. 40   Thomas Mitchell, *Three Expeditions into the Interior of Eastern Australia* (vol. 1), London: T. & W. Boone, 1838.

p. 42   Brian Saunders, *Discovery of Australia's Fishes: A History of Australian Ichthyology to 1930*, Canberra: CSIRO Publishing, 2014, pp. 15–9, 67–72, 98; Daniel Pauly, *Darwin's Fishes: An Encyclopedia of Ichthyology, Ecology, and Evolution*, Cambridge: Cambridge University Press, 2007.

Chapter 3

p. 45   Garry Kerr, *Craft and Craftsmen of Australian Fishing 1870–1970*, Portland: Mains'l Books, 1985, p. 213; R. C. J. Lenanton, 'The Commercial Fisheries of Temperate Western Australian Estuaries: Early Settlement to 1975', North Beach, WA: Western Australian Marine Research Laboratories, Department of Fisheries and Wildlife, 1984.

p. 47   Kerr, *Craft and Craftsmen of Australian Fishing 1870–1970*, p. 34; *Report of the Royal Commission Appointed on the 8th January, to Inquire into and Report on the Fisheries of this Colony*, Sydney: Thomas Richards, Government Printer, 1880, p. 12; Anne Jacobsen, 'Steam Trawling on the Southeast Continental Shelf of Australia: An Environmental History of Fishing, Management and Science in NSW, 1865–1961', PhD thesis, School of Geography and Environmental Studies, University of Tasmania, 2010, p. 51.

Endnotes

p. 47   Julian Edmund Tenison-Woods, *Fish and Fisheries of New South Wales*, Sydney: Government Printer, 1883, pp. 34, 128.

p. 47   Callum Roberts, *The Unnatural History of the Sea*, Washington, DC: Island Press/Shearwater Books, 2007, p. 48.

p. 47   Richard White, *The Organic Machine*, New York: Hill and Wang, c. 1995; Mark Kurlansky, *Cod: A Biography of a Fish that Changed the World*, New York: Walker and Co., 1997.

p. 48   *The Industrial Progress of New South Wales*, Sydney: Thomas Richards, Government Printer, 1871, p. 788; Anthony J. Harrison, 'The Fisheries Savant: William Saville-Kent in Victoria, 1887–8', *Historical Records of Australian Science*, vol. 11, no. 3, 1997, p. 423.

p. 48   Nigel Isaacs, 'Sydney's First Ice', *Dictionary of Sydney*, 2011: dictionaryofsydney.org/entry/sydneys_first_ice (accessed 13 April 2023); Alistair Bowen, 'Material Evidence for Early Commercial Fishing Activities on the Far South Coast of New South Wales', *Australasian Historical Archaeology*, vol. 22, 2004, pp. 79–89.

p. 48   *The Industrial Progress of New South Wales*, p. 784; Evelyn Wallace-Carter, *For They Were Fishers*, Adelaide: Amphrite Publishing House, 1987, p. 8.

p. 48   *Report of the Royal Commission Appointed on the 8th January*, p. 29.

p. 48   David Stead from the New South Wales Fisheries Branch, 1912: Cited in Jacobsen, 'Steam Trawling on the South-east Continental Shelf of Australia', pp. 99–100.

pp. 48–9 Wallace-Carter, *For They Were Fishers*, p. 8; *The Industrial Progress of New South Wales*, p. 784; Bowen, 'Material Evidence for Early Commercial Fishing Activities', p. 83.

p. 49   'The Australian Herring', *The Shoalhaven Telegraph*, 11 July 1896, p. 2.

p. 49   Kerr, *Craft and Craftsmen of Australian Fishing 1870–1970*, p. 20.

p. 49   Alistair Bowen, 'The Central Role of Chinese People in Australia's Colonial Fishing Industry', *Journal of Australian Colonial History*, vol. 12, 2010, pp. 97–118; Alistair Bowen, 'Dating a Chinese Fish Curing Camp at Port Albert, Victoria', *The Artefact*, vol. 30, 2007, pp. 4–30; Lindsay Thompson, *History of the Fisheries of New South Wales: With a Sketch of the Laws by which They Have Been Regulated*, Sydney: Government Printer, 1893, pp. 2–3. See also: Ian Hoskins, *Coast*, Sydney: NewSouth Publishing, 2013, pp. 149–51; David Martin,

'Northern Territory Fishing History Traced', *Feedstuffs*, vol. 72, no. 5, 2000, p. 13; David Martin, 'Northern Territory Fisheries Expanding', *Feedstuffs*, vol. 72, no. 5, 2000, p. 12.

p. 50　*The Industrial Progress of New South Wales*, pp. 785, 789; see also: Hoskins, *Coast*, p. 155.

p. 50　Wallace-Carter, *For They Were Fishers*, p. 40.

p. 51　Hoskins, *Coast*, pp. 161–82; John Newton, *A Savage History of Whaling in the Pacific and Southern Oceans*, Sydney: NewSouth Publishing, 2013.

p. 51　Noel Haysom, *Trawlers, Trollers and Trepangers: The Story of the Queensland Commercial Fishing Industry pre-1988*, Brisbane: QLD Department of Primary Industries, 2001, pp. 18–30; Martin, 'Northern Territory Fisheries Expanding', p. 12; Martin, 'Northern Territory Fishing History Traced', p. 13.

p. 51　J. G. Pepperell, 'The Good Old Days? Historical Insights into Coastal NSW Fish Populations and their Fisheries', Sydney: The NSW Recreational Fishing Trusts Expenditure Committee, N.D., p. 42; Kerr, *Craft and Craftsmen of Australian Fishing 1870–1970*, pp. 68–9; John Wilkinson, 'Commercial Fishing in NSW: Origins and Developments to the Early 1990s', Sydney: NSW Parliamentary Library Research Service, 1997, p. 16.

p. 51　Haysom, *Trawlers, Trollers and Trepangers*, pp. 5–9.

p. 54　Wallace-Carter, *For They Were Fishers*, p. 49.

p. 54　ibid.; Haysom, *Trawlers, Trollers and Trepangers*, p. 5; 'An Act to Regulate Oyster Fisheries and to Encourage the Formation of Oyster-beds, 1st February, 1868': legislation.nsw.gov.au/view/pdf/asmade/act-1868-3a (accessed 13 April 2023).

p. 54　'Oyster Fisheries', *The Sydney Mail and New South Wales Advertiser*, 9 September 1871, p. 893.

p. 54　Thompson, *History of the Fisheries of New South Wales*, p. 52.

p. 55　William Saville-Kent, 'Oysters in Australasia–I', *Brisbane Courier*, 20 January 1891, p. 6.

p. 55　Chris L. Gillies et al., 'Australian Shellfish Ecosystems: Past Distribution, Current Status and Future Direction', *PLOS ONE*, vol. 13, no. 2, 2018, pp. 13–14.

p. 55　Wallace-Carter, *For They Were Fishers*, p. 12.

Endnotes

p. 55   Bowen, 'Material Evidence for Early Commercial Fishing Activities',
        p. 83; Kerr, *Craft and Craftsmen of Australian Fishing 1870–1970*; *Report
        of the Royal Commission Appointed on the 8th January*, p. 53.

p. 56   Pat Clifford, 'Australian Fishing Industry – Interviews with New
        South Wales Fishermen', State Library of New South Wales, MLOH
        277/9, 1990; Bowen, 'Material Evidence for Early Commercial
        Fishing Activities', p. 82; John Clarke, *Old Salt*, Sydney: Royal
        Australian Historical Society, 2011, p. 43; Kerr, *Craft and Craftsmen
        of Australian Fishing 1870–1970*, p. 26.

p. 56   Roberts, *The Unnatural History of the Sea*, p. 147; Kerr, *Craft and
        Craftsmen of Australian Fishing 1870–1970*, pp. 23, 26, 34.

p. 57   Stuart Rowland, 'Overview of the History, Fishery, Biology and
        Aquaculture of Murray Cod (Maccullochella peelii peelii)', Manage-
        ment of Murray Cod in the Murray–Darling Basin Workshop, 3–4
        June 2004, Canberra, Murray–Darling Basin Commission, p. 42.

p. 57   *The Voyage of Governor Phillip to Botany Bay: With an Account of the
        Establishment of the Colonies of Port Jackson and Norfolk Island*, Sydney:
        University of Sydney Library, 2003, p. 77; Stephen Gapps, 'Finding
        Bloody Point', *The Sydney Wars*, 11 March 2019: thesydneywars.
        com/2019/03/11/finding-bloody-point/ (accessed 3 April 2023);
        Stephen Gapps, *The Sydney Wars*, Sydney: NewSouth Publishing,
        2018, pp. 25–27.

p. 57   Grace Karskens, 'Barangaroo and the Eora Fisherwomen', *Dictionary
        of Sydney*: dictionaryofsydney.org/entry/barangaroo_and_the_eora_
        fisherwomen (accessed 26 April 2023).

p. 58   Ben Collins, 'Reconciling the Dark History of Slavery and Murder
        in Australian Pearling, Points to a Brighter Future', *ABC News*,
        Australian Broadcasting Corporation, 9 September 2018.

p. 58   Hoskins, *Coast*, p. 161; Danielle Clode, *Killers in Eden: The True Story of
        Killer Whales and their Remarkable Partnership with the Whalers of Twofold
        Bay*, Crows Nest, NSW: Allen & Unwin, 2002.

p. 59   Bowen, 'Material Evidence for Early Commercial Fishing Activities',
        pp. 92–4.

p. 59   ibid., pp. 86, 92; Jillian Barnes, 'Aboriginal Cultural Tourism:
        Enterprise, Contested Mobilities and Negotiating a Responsible
        Australian Travel Culture', *Journal of Australian Indigenous Issues*,

vol. 18, no. 1, 2015, pp. 116–42; Richard Strauss, 'The Outdoor Living Supplement: Outdoor Recreation in Post-War Sydney 1945–1975', PhD thesis, History, Macquarie University, 2007, p. 189.

p. 59   Bowen, 'Material Evidence for Early Commercial Fishing Activities', pp. 80–1.

p. 59   Thompson, *History of the Fisheries of New South Wales*, p. 26.

pp. 59–60 *The Industrial Progress of New South Wales*, p. 787.

p. 60   'Oyster Fisheries', *The Sydney Mail and New South Wales Advertiser*, 9 September 1871, p. 893.

p. 60   *Report of the Royal Commission Appointed on the 8th January*, p. 81.

p. 60   Tenison-Woods, *Fish and Fisheries of New South Wales*, p. 128.

p. 60   Roberts, *The Unnatural History of the Sea*, p. 164; Ruth Thurston et al., 'Origins of the Bottom Trawling Controversy in the British Isles: 19th Century Witness Testimonies Reveal Evidence of Early Fishery Declines', *Fish and Fisheries*, vol. 15, no. 3, 2014, pp. 506–22.

p. 60   Thompson, *History of the Fisheries of New South Wales*, p. 26; *The Industrial Progress of New South Wales*, p. 787; *Report of the Royal Commission Appointed on the 8th January*, pp. 53, 81; Jacobsen, 'Steam Trawling on the South-east Continental Shelf of Australia', ch.2; Andrea Gaynor, 'Shifting Baselines or Shifting Currents? An Environmental History of Fish and Fishing in the South-west Capes Region of Western Australia', in J. Christensen and M. Tull (eds), *Historical Perspectives of Fisheries Exploitation in the Indo-Pacific*, New York: Springer, 2006, p. 236; Anthony J. Harrison, 'The Fisheries Savant: William Saville-Kent in Victoria, 1887–8', *Historical Records of Australian Science*, vol. 11, no. 3, 1997, pp. 419–29; David Harris, '"It's just fly fishing against net fishing . . .": Commercial Fishing, Angling and the Gippsland Lakes, 1870s, 1880s', in E. Eklund and J. Fenley (eds), *Earth and Industry: Stories from Gippsland*, Melbourne: Monash University Press, 2015, pp. 124–45.

Chapter 4

p. 64   'Fishing', *The Yeoman, and Australian Acclimatiser*, 5 September 1863, p. 774; Izaak Walton, *The Compleat Angler or, The Contemplative Man's Recreation: Being a Discourse of Fish & Fishing not Unworthy the Perusal of Most Anglers*, New York: Hodder & Stoughton, 1911.

Endnotes

p. 64   Horace William Wheelwright, *Natural History Sketches*, London: Frederick Warne, 1871, pp. 246–7.

p. 65   Bob Dunn, *Angling in Australia: Its History and Writings*, Balmain, NSW: David Ell Press, 1991, p. 82.

p. 65   Claire Brennan, 'Imperial Game: A History of Hunting, Society, Exotic Species and the Environment in New Zealand and Victoria 1840–1901', PhD thesis, Department of History, University of Melbourne, 2004, pp. 12, 146.

p. 66   Arthur Nicols, *The Acclimatisation of the Salmonidae at the Antipodes: Its History and Results*, London: Sampson Low, Marston Searle & Rivington, 1882, p. 2.

p. 66   Jean Walker, *Origins of the Tasmanian Trout*, Hobart, Tasmania: Inland Fisheries Commission, 1988, pp. 11–25; Adrian Franklin, 'Performing Acclimatisation: The Agency of Trout Fishing in Postcolonial Australia', *Ethnos*, vol. 76, no. 1, 2011, pp. 25–6.

pp. 66–7 Arthur Nicols, *The Acclimatisation of the Salmonidae at the Antipodes: Its History and Results*, pp. 1–2.

p. 67   Walker, *Origins of the Tasmanian Trout*, pp. 25, 37–8; Franklin, 'Performing Acclimatisation, pp. 25–6; A. M. Clayton, *New South Wales Rod Fishers' Society: The First 75 Years*, Sydney: The Society, 1978, p. 4.

p. 68   Peter Minard, 'Salmonid Acclimatisation in Colonial Victoria: Improvement, Restoration and Recreation 1858–1909', *Environment and History*, vol. 21, no. 2, 2015, pp. 179–99.

p. 68   Anthony J. Harrison, 'The Fisheries Savant: William Saville-Kent in Victoria, 1887–8', *Historical Records of Australian Science*, vol. 11, no. 3, 1997, p. 422.

pp. 68–9 Richard White, *On Holidays: A History of Getting Away in Australia*, Melbourne: Pluto Press, 2005, pp. 54–69.

p. 69   Peter Gibson (ed.), *The Flowing Stream: 100 Years of Angling with the New South Wales Rod Fishers' Society*, Paddington, NSW: Creek of Peace, 2004, p. vii.

p. 69   Franklin, 'Performing Acclimatisation', pp. 24–6; John Hedge, *Trout Fishing in New South Wales*, Sydney: Abbey Publishing Co., 1962, p. 11.

p. 69   Hedge, *Trout Fishing in New South Wales*, pp. 59–60.

p. 70   Brennan, 'Imperial Game', p. 210.

p. 70   Gibson (ed.), *The Flowing Stream*, p. 12.

p. 70　William Senior, *Travel and Trout in the Antipodes: An Angler's Sketches in Tasmania and New Zealand*, London: Chatto and Windus, 1880, pp. 155–8.

p. 71　Franklin, 'Performing Acclimatisation', pp. 27–9.

p. 71　James Woodford, 'Advance Australia Green', *Griffith Review*, vol. 19, 2008, p. 189.

p. 72　Douglas Stewart, *Fishing Around the Monaro: A Selection from the Seven Rivers*, Canberra: Australian National University Press, 1978, p. 36.

p. 72　'A Western Tourist Centre', *The Sydney Morning Herald*, 31 October 1905, p. 6.

pp. 72–3　Susan Lawler, 'Rabbits of the River: Trout are Not Native to Australia', *The Conversation*, 13 May 2013: theconversation.com/rabbits-of-the-river-trout-are-not-native-to-australia-14115 (accessed 13 April 2023); Woodford, 'Advance Australia Green', pp. 189–90.

p. 73　Tarmo A. Raadik, 'Recovery Actions for Seven Endemic and Threatened Victorian Galaxiid Species', Victoria: Department of Environment, Land, Water and Planning, 2019; Bridie Smith, 'Trout Moved Out to Give Galaxias Breathing Space', *The Age*, 9 May 2013.

Chapter 5

p. 77　Ruth Thurston et al., 'Nineteenth Century Narratives Reveal Historic Catch Rates for Australian Snapper (*Pagrus Auratus*)', *Fish and Fisheries*, vol. 17, no. 1, pp. 1–16; J. Thornton-Champley, *Tales of Australian Angling*, Melbourne: A. H. Massina & Co., Printers, 1912, p. 5; Bob Dunn, *Angling in Australia: Its History and Writings*, Balmain, NSW: David Ell Press, 1991.

p. 79　Frederick G. Aflalo, *A Sketch of the Natural History of Australia: With Some Notes on Sport*, London: MacMillan and Co., 1896. pp. 203–6; Thornton-Champley, *Tales of Australian Angling*, p. 5; J. Thornton-Champley, *Australian Angler's Guide and Sea-fisher's Manual*, Melbourne: G. Robertson, c. 1910, p. 146.

p. 80　Richard White, *Inventing Australia*, Sydney: George Allen and Unwin, 1981, ch. 6.

p. 80　Thornton-Champley, *Australian Angler's Guide and Sea-fisher's Manual*, p. 75.

Endnotes

p. 80   Aflalo, *A Sketch of the Natural History of Australia*, p. 201; Caroline Ford, *Sydney Beaches: A History*, Sydney: NewSouth Publishing, 2014.

p. 81   Charles Thackeray, *The Amateur Fisherman's Guide*, Sydney: George Robertson & Co., 1895, p. 3; Aflalo, *A Sketch of the Natural History of Australia*, p. 213.

p. 81   Dunn, *Angling in Australia*, p. 107.

p. 81   Thackeray, *The Amateur Fisherman's Guide*, p. 3.

p. 84   ibid., p. 4; 'A Fishing Party's Experience', *The Chronicle* (Adelaide) 14 March 1903, p. 39; 'A Piscatorial Pleasure Party', *Illustrated Sydney News and New South Wales Agriculturalist and Grazier*, 31 March 1876, p. 15.

p. 84   Lachlan Macquarie, *Diary 11 March 1821 – 12 February 1822*, Lachlan and Elizabeth Macquarie Archive, Macquarie University: mq.edu. au/maquarie-archive/lema/1821/1821apr.html (accessed 27 April 2023); Claire Brennan, 'Imperial Game: A History of Hunting, Society, Exotic Species and the Environment in New Zealand and Victoria 1840–1901', PhD thesis, Department of History, University of Melbourne, 2004, p. 72.

p. 84   Thackeray, *The Amateur Fisherman's Guide*, p. 6.

p. 85   Thornton-Champley, *Australian Angler's Guide*, pp. 1–4; Thackeray, *The Amateur Fisherman's Guide*; Frederick G. Aflalo, *Sea-fish: An Account of the Methods of Angling as Practised on the English Coast, with Notes on the Capture of the more Sporting Fishes in Continental, South African, and Australian Waters*, London: George Routledge and Sons, c. 1904, pp. 244–7.

p. 86   Thornton-Champley, *The Australian Angler's Guide*, pp. 100–1.

p. 86   Aflalo, *A Sketch of the Natural History of Australia*, p. 207; Thackeray, *The Amateur Fisherman's Guide*, p. 12.

p. 86   Thackeray, *The Amateur Fisherman's Guide*, p. 10.

pp. 86–7 Aflalo, *Sea-fish*, pp. 93–4.

p. 87   Thackeray, *The Amateur Fisherman's Guide*, p. 30.

p. 87   Aflalo, *A Sketch of the Natural History of Australia*, pp. 200, 209.

p. 88   Thackeray, *The Amateur Fisherman's Guide*, p. 28.

p. 88   John Cameron, *The Fisherman: A Guide to the Inexperienced: How, When and Where to Catch Fish*, Brisbane: Gordon & Gotch, 1888, p. 68.

p. 89   Pat Clifford, 'Australian Fishing Industry – Interviews with New

South Wales Fishermen', State Library of New South Wales, MLOH 277/9, 1990.

p. 89   Stuart Rowland, 'Overview of the History, Fishery, Biology and Aquaculture of Murray Cod (Maccullochella peelii peelii)', Management of Murray Cod in the Murray–Darling Basin Workshop, 3–4 June 2004, Canberra, Murray–Darling Basin Commission, p. 39; W. G. Noble, 'Murray Cod' (letter to the editor), *Sydney Morning Herald*, 6 October 1955, p. 2.

p. 89   Cameron, *The Fisherman*, p. 68; Thurstan et al., 'Nineteenth Century Narratives Reveal Historic Catch Rates for Australian Snapper', p. 6.

p. 90   Thornton-Champley, *Australian Angler's Guide*, p. 111.

p. 90   Dunn, *Angling in Australia*, p. 109.

p. 90   ibid., pp. 110, 113; Bill Garner, *Born in a Tent: How Camping Makes Us Australian*, Sydney: NewSouth Publishing, 2013, pp. 134–7; Michael McGhie, 'Fishing the Peel-Harvey Estuary', *Friends of Mandurah Community Museum Newsletter*, October 2010, p. 5.

p. 91   Thornton-Champley, *Australian Angler's Guide*, p. 143.

p. 92   A. M. Clayton, *New South Wales Rod Fishers' Society: The First 75 Years*, Sydney: The Society, 1978, p. 1; Dunn, *Angling in Australia*, pp. 119, 124–5; 'Amateur Fishermen's Association of New South Wales', *Sydney Morning Herald*, 20 February 1895, p. 5.

Chapter 6

p. 97   Anne Jacobsen, 'Steam Trawling on the South-east Continental Shelf of Australia: An Environmental History of Fishing, Management and Science in NSW, 1865–1961', PhD thesis, School of Geography and Environmental Studies, University of Tasmania, 2010, p. 99.

p. 97   Dulcie Stace, 'Australian Fishing Industry – Interviews with New South Wales fishermen', State Library of New South Wales, MLOH 277/9, 1990; Brian Egloff, *Wreck Bay: An Aboriginal Fishing Community*, Canberra: Aboriginal Studies Press, 1990, p. 39.

p. 97   Garry Kerr, *Craft and Craftsmen of Australian Fishing 1870–1970*, Portland: Mains'l Books, 1985, pp. 68–9.

p. 97   ibid., p. 187.

p. 98   John Wilkinson, 'Commercial Fishing in NSW: Origins and Developments to the Early 1990s', Sydney: NSW Parliamentary Library Research Service, 1997, pp. 11, 18–9.

Endnotes

p. 98   Kerr, *Craft and Craftsmen of Australian Fishing 1870–1970*, p. 225.

p. 98   Wilkinson, 'Commercial Fishing in NSW', pp. 18–9; Kerr, *Craft and Craftsmen of Australian Fishing 1870–1970*, pp. 187, 225.

p. 99   Kerr, *Craft and Craftsmen of Australian Fishing 1870–1970*, pp. 31, 51.

p. 99   Jacobsen, 'Steam Trawling on the South-east Continental Shelf of Australia', pp. 120–8; Wilkinson, 'Commercial Fishing in NSW', p. 19; Harald Dannevig, *Fisheries: Notes on Australia's Fisheries with a Summary of the Results Obtained by the F.I.S. 'Endeavour'*, Melbourne: Department of Trade and Customs, 1913.

p. 100 Jacobsen, 'Steam Trawling on the South-east Continental Shelf of Australia', p. 146.

p. 100 Chris Grieve and Geoff Richard, 'Recent History of Australia's South East Fishery: A Manager's Perspective', *Marine & Freshwater Research*, vol. 52, 2001, p. 377; Jacobsen, 'Steam Trawling on the South-east Continental Shelf of Australia'; Pamela Hale and Paul Ashton, *Raising the Nation: A History of Commonwealth Departments of Agriculture, Fisheries and Forestry, 1901–2001*, Canberra: Department of Agriculture, Forestry and Fisheries, 2002, pp. 112–3.

p. 100 Wilkinson, 'Commercial Fishing in NSW', p. 18.

p. 101 E. J. Ferguson Wood, 'The Canning of Fish and Fish Products in Australia', *Fisheries Circular*, no. 2, 1940, p. 43; Wilkinson, 'Commercial Fishing in NSW', p. 19; John Little, *Down to the Sea: The True Saga of an Australian Fishing Dynasty*, Sydney: MacMillan, 2004.

pp. 101–2 T. C. Roughley, *Fish and Fisheries of Australia*, Sydney: Angus & Robertson, 1951, pp. 241–2.

p. 102 'Turning Turtle into Canned Delicacies', *The Daily News*, 11 October 1923, p. 11; 'Turtle Products', *The West Australian*, 10 October 1923, p. 7.

p. 102 Brooke Halkyard, 'Exploiting Green and Hawksbill Turtles in Western Australia: The Commercial Marine Turtle Fishery', in J. Christensen and M. Tull (eds), *Historical Perspectives of Fisheries Exploitation in the Indo-Pacific*, New York: Springer, 2006, pp. 213–6; E. M. Noblet, *The Winds that Blew at Cossack*, Sydney: Angus & Robertson, 1968, pp. 31–3. For a discussion of other fisheries, see also: Ben Daley et al., 'Exploiting Marine Wildlife in Queensland: The Commercial Dugong and Marine Turtle Fisheries, 1847–1969', *Australian Economic History Review*, vol. 48, no. 3, 2008, pp. 227–65.

p. 103 Evelyn Wallace-Carter, *For They Were Fishers*, Adelaide: Amphrite Publishing House, 1987, pp. 253–6.

pp. 103–4 Grieve and Richard, 'Recent History of Australia's South East Fishery', p. 377.

p. 104 Richard J. Gowers, 'Selling the "Untold Wealth" in the Seas: A Social and Cultural History of the South-east Australian Shelf Trawling Industry, 1915–1961', *Environment and History*, vol. 14, no. 2, 2000, pp. 266–75; Jacobsen, 'Steam Trawling on the South-east Continental Shelf of Australia', pp. 200–1; N. L. Klaer, 'Steam Trawl Catches from South-eastern Australia from 1918 to 1957: Trends in Catch Rates and Species Composition', *Marine and Freshwater Research*, vol. 52, no. 4, 2001, pp. 399–410; Michael Puglisi and Natalina Puglisi, *Harvesting the Sea: The Story of the Puglisi Family, Fishing Pioneers*, Gordon, NSW: Mini-Publishing, 2009, p. 135.

p. 104 Jacobsen, 'Steam Trawling on the South-east Continental Shelf of Australia', p. 163.

p. 104 Grieve and Richard, 'Recent History of Australia's South East Fishery', p. 422.

p. 104 Jacobsen, 'Steam Trawling on the South-east Continental Shelf of Australia', pp. 35–6.

p. 104 Grieve and Richard, 'Recent History of Australia's South East Fishery', p. 377.

p. 105 Jacobsen, 'Steam Trawling on the South-east Continental Shelf of Australia', pp. 210–26; Wilkinson, 'Commercial Fishing in NSW', pp. 30, 31.

p. 105 'Big Tuna: The Problem of Where They Go', *Australian Fisheries*, vol. 1, no. 1, 1941–2, p. 3.

p. 106 Callum Roberts, *The Unnatural History of the Sea*, Washington, DC: Island Press/Shearwater Books, 2007, p. 327.

p. 106 Pascale Baelde, 'Fishers' Description of Changes in Fishing Gear and Fishing Practices in the Australian South East Trawl Fishery', *Marine and Freshwater Research*, vol. 52, no. 4, 2001, p. 412; Puglisi and Puglisi, *Harvesting the Sea*, pp. 149, 350, 406.

p. 106 Noel Haysom, *Trawlers, Trollers and Trepangers: The Story of the Queensland Commercial Fishing Industry pre-1988*, Brisbane: QLD Department of Primary Industries, 2001, p. 35.

Endnotes

p. 106 R. D. J. Tilzey and K. R. Rowling, 'History of Australia's South East Fishery: A Scientist's Perspective', *Marine & Freshwater Research*, vol. 52, no. 4, 2001, p. 361.

p. 106 'Filleting Machine Developed', *Australian Fisheries*, vol. 29, no. 9, 1970, p. 27.

p. 107 Puglisi and Puglisi, *Harvesting the Sea*, p. 295.

p. 107 Wilkinson, 'Commercial Fishing in NSW', pp. 30, 31.

p. 107 John Wilkinson, 'NSW Fishing Industry: Changes and Challenges in the Twenty-First Century', NSW Parliamentary Library: Briefing Paper No 11/04, 2004, p. 2.

p. 108 CCSBT Extended Scientific Committee, 'Report on Biology, Stock Status and Management of Southern Bluefin Tuna: 2022', Canberra: Commission for the Conservation of Southern Bluefin Tuna, 2022: ccsbt.org/sites/default/files/userfiles/file/docs_english/meetings/meeting_reports/ccsbt_29/ESC27_Attachment_07_ReportOn BiologyStatusManagement.pdf (accessed 4 April 2023); Sid Adams, 'Southern Bluefin Tuna: A Contested History', in J. Christensen and M. Tull (eds), *Historical Perspectives of Fisheries Exploitation in the Indo-Pacific*, New York: Springer, 2006, p. 175.

p. 108 Stuart Rowland, 'Overview of the History, Fishery, Biology and Aquaculture of Murray Cod (Maccullochella peelii peelii)', Management of Murray Cod in the Murray–Darling Basin Workshop, 3–4 June 2004, Canberra, Murray–Darling Basin Commission, p. 38.

p. 108 'Ulladulla Fishermen See Troubled Waters Ahead', *Australian Fisheries*, vol. 49, no. 4, 1990, pp. 22–4.

p. 108 Ken Tidswell, 'Australian Fishing Industry – Interviews with New South Wales Fishermen', State Library of New South Wales, MLOH 277/9, 1990.

p. 108 Sarah Drummond, *Salt Story: Of Sea-Dogs and Fisherwomen*, Fremantle: Fremantle Press, 2014.

p. 109 'Australia Seeks Right of Coastal States to Establish Fishery Zones', *Australian Fisheries*, vol. 30, no. 9, 1971, pp. 9–11.

p. 110 Cited in Roberts, *The Unnatural History of the Sea*, p. 291.

p. 111 Australian Fisheries Management Authority, 'Gemfish' (2023): afma.gov.au/species/gemfish#referenced-section-1 (accessed 13 April 2013).

p. 112 Puglisi and Puglisi, *Harvesting the Sea*, pp. 444–5.

p. 112 Baelde, 'Fishers' Description of Changes in Fishing Gear and Fishing Practices', pp. 411, 414; 'Ulladulla Fishermen See Troubled Waters Ahead', pp. 22–4.

p. 112 Wilkinson, 'NSW Fishing Industry: Changes and Challenges', p. 29.

p. 112 Puglisi and Puglisi, *Harvesting the Sea*, pp. 446–50.

Chapter 7

p. 116 Jodi Frawley, 'Kissing Fish: Rex Hunt, Popular Culture, Sustainability and Fishing Practices', *Journal of Australian Studies*, vol. 39, no. 3, 2015, p. 320; Richard Strauss, 'The Outdoor Living Supplement: Outdoor Recreation in Post-War Sydney 1945–1975', PhD thesis, History, Macquarie University, 2007, p. 288.

p. 117 Bob Dunn, *Angling in Australia: Its History and Writings*, Balmain, NSW: David Ell Press, 1991, p. 140; Richard White, *On Holidays: A History of Getting Away in Australia*, Melbourne: Pluto Press, 2005, pp. 124–5.

p. 117 'Nature and Leisure', *The Australian Rod & Gun*, vol. 3, no. 3, 1950, p. 19.

p. 117 'Aboriginal People Living and Working on the NSW Coast: A Historical Review', Sydney: Office of Environment and Heritage NSW, 2012, pp. 27, 32; Brian Egloff, *Wreck Bay: An Aboriginal Fishing Community*, Canberra: Aboriginal Studies Press, 1990, pp. 48–9.

pp. 117–8 Wal Hardy, 'The Xmas Angle', *Australian Outdoors & Fishing*, vol. 14, no. 2, 1955, p. 31.

p. 118 'The Jaws of Death', *The Australian Angler*, vol. 1, no. 1, 1969, pp. 12–15, 49.

p. 118 Anthony James, 'I Remember the Day', *The Australian Angler*, vol. 1, no. 12, 1971, pp. 18–19, 40.

p. 119 Strauss, 'The Outdoor Living Supplement', p. 8; White, *On Holidays*, p. 142.

p. 119 Alison Cadzow et al., *Waterborne: Vietnamese Australians and Sydney's Georges River Parks and Green Spaces*, Sydney: UTS ePress, 2011, pp. 28–9.

p. 119 Dunn, *Angling in Australia*, p. 140; Frawley, 'Kissing Fish', p. 320; Gary W. Henry and Jeremy M. Lyle, *The National Recreational and Indigenous Fishing Survey*, Canberra: Australian Government Department of Agriculture, Fisheries and Forestry, 2003, p. 13.

Endnotes

p. 120 Henry and Lyle, *The National Recreational and Indigenous Fishing Survey*, p. 13; Tess Travers, 'For the Girls', *Outdoors and Fishing*, vol. 11, no. 6, 1953, p. 399.

p. 121 Henry and Lyle, *The National Recreational and Indigenous Fishing Survey*.

p. 122 K. C. G. Ashby, 'Apathetic Anglers', *Australian Sportfishing*, vol. 1, no. 4, 1969, p. 67.

p. 123 'N.S.W. Scientist to Study Anglers' Problems', *Australian Fisheries*, vol. 30, no. 12, 1971, p. 2; Soros-Longworth & McKenzie, 'Effects of Water Borne Traffic on the Environment of the Hawkesbury River', Sydney: Department of Public Works, 1977, p. 11; Strauss, 'The Outdoor Living Supplement', p. 147.

p. 123 A. Steffe and D. Chapman, 'A Survey of Daytime Recreational Fishing During the Annual Period, March 1999 to February 2000, in Lake Macquarie', New South Wales: NSW Fisheries, 2003; Salim Momtaz and William Gladstone, 'Ban on Commercial Fishing in the Estuarine Waters of New South Wales, Australia: Community Consultation and Social Impacts', *Environmental Impact Assessment Review*, vol. 28, no. 2–3, 2008, pp. 214–25.

p. 123 John Wilkinson, 'NSW Fishing Industry: Changes and Challenges in the Twenty-First Century', NSW Parliamentary Library: Briefing Paper No. 11/04, 2004, p. 34; Momtaz and Gladstone, 'Ban on Commercial Fishing in the Estuarine Waters of New South Wales', p. 214.

p. 123 Wilkinson, 'NSW Fishing Industry', pp. 37–8; Momtaz and Gladstone, 'Ban on Commercial Fishing in the Estuarine Waters of New South Wales', p. 214.

p. 124 'Northern Territory Barramundi Fishery Environmental Management System', Darwin: Northern Territory Seafood Council, 2010, p. 6; Paul Toohey, 'Catch Cry', *The Bulletin*, 18 January 2005, p. 42.

p. 124 Toohey, 'Catch Cry', *The Bulletin*, 18 January 2005, pp. 41–2.

p. 124 Henry and Lyle, *The National Recreational and Indigenous Fishing Survey*, p. 13; B. E. Malseed and N. R. Sumner, 'A 12-month Survey of Recreational Fishing in the Swan-Canning Estuary Basin of Western Australia during 1998–99', *Fisheries Research Report*, no. 126, Perth: WA Marine Research Laboratories, Fisheries Research Division, 2001.

p. 124 Kristin Kleisner et al., 'Australia: Reconstructing Estimates of Total Fisheries Removal, 1950–2010', *Working Paper Series*, Fisheries Centre, University of British Columbia, 2015, p. 3; D. P. McPhee et al., 'Swallowing the Bait: Is Recreational Fishing in Australia Ecologically Sustainable?', *Pacific Conservation Biology*, vol. 8, 2004, p. 42; Joseph Christensen and Gary Jackson, 'Shark Bay Snapper: Science, Policy, and the Decline of and Recovery of a Marine Recreational Fishery', in J. Christensen and M. Tull (eds), *Historical Perspectives of Fisheries Exploitation in the Indo-Pacific*, New York: Springer, 2006, p. 252.

p. 124 Matthew Young et al., 'Impacts of Recreational Fishing in Australia: Historical Declines, Self-regulation and Evidence of an Early Warning System', *Environmental Conservation*, vol. 41, no. 4, 2014, p. 351.

pp. 124–5 Ruth Thurston et al., 'Nineteenth Century Narratives Reveal Historic Catch Rates for Australian Snapper (*Pagrus Auratus*)', *Fish and Fisheries*, vol. 17, no. 1, p. 10.

p. 125 Frawley, 'Kissing Fish', p. 315.

pp. 125–6 ibid., p. 310. See also: Jodi Frawley, Scott Nichols, Heather Goodall and Liz Baker, *Talking Fish: Making Connections with the Rivers of the Murray–Darling Basin*, Canberra: Murray–Darling Basin Authority, 2012.

p. 126 Frawley, 'Kissing Fish', pp. 309–10; Young et al., 'Impacts of Recreational Fishing in Australia', p. 353; Lance Ferris, 'Fishing's Poisoned Barb', *Australian Geographic*, vol. 74, 2004, p. 32.

p. 127 McPhee et al., 'Swallowing the Bait', p. 42; Henry and Lyle, *The National Recreational and Indigenous Fishing Survey*, pp. 13, 65; Frawley, 'Kissing Fish', pp. 319–20.

p. 127 Noel Haysom, *Trawlers, Trollers and Trepangers: The Story of the Queensland Commercial Fishing Industry pre-1988*, Brisbane: QLD Department of Primary Industries, 2001, p. 35.

p. 127 McPhee et al., 'Swallowing the Bait', p. 46; Prabha Prayaga et al., 'The Value of Recreational Fishing in the Great Barrier Reef, Australia: A Pooled Revealed Preference and Contingent Behaviour Model', *Marine Policy*, vol. 34, no. 2, 2010, p. 244.

Endnotes

pp. 127–8 Toohey, 'Catch Cry', p. 44; Christensen and Jackson, 'Shark Bay Snapper', pp. 251–68.

p. 128 McPhee et al., 'Swallowing the Bait', p. 46; Prayaga et al., 'The Value of Recreational Fishing in the Great Barrier Reef, Australia', p. 244; Frawley, 'Kissing Fish', pp. 307–8.

p. 128 McPhee et al., 'Swallowing the Bait', p. 42; Frawley, 'Kissing Fish', pp. 307–8; Michelle Voyer, '"It's part of me": Understanding the Values, Images and Principles of Coastal Users and their Influence on the Social Acceptability of MPAs', *Marine Policy*, vol. 52, 2015, p. 101.

pp. 128–9 'Anglers Slam Labor over Sydney Lock-outs', *Fishing World Magazine*, 2 October 2014: fishingworld.com.au/news/anglers-slam-labor-over-sydney-lock-outs (accessed 13 April 2023).

p. 130 Henry and Lyle, *The National Recreational and Indigenous Fishing Survey*.

p. 130 Janet Hunt, 'The NSW Government Needs to Stop Prosecuting Aboriginal Fishers if it Really Wants to Close the Gap', *The Conversation*, 11 October 2021: theconversation.com/the-nsw-government-needs-to-stop-prosecuting-aboriginal-fishers-if-it-really-wants-to-close-the-gap-168749 (accessed 2 February 2023).

p. 130 Lisa Palmer, 'Fishing Lifestyles: "Territorians", Traditional Owners and the Management of Recreational Fishing in Kakadu National Park', *Australian Geographical Studies*, vol. 42, no. 1, 2004, p. 71; 'Aboriginal Women's Heritage: Port Stephens', Sydney: Department of Environment and Conservation NSW, 2004, pp. 47–8; Henry and Lyle, *The National Recreational and Indigenous Fishing Survey*, p. 14; Sandy Toussaint, 'Fishing for Fish and for Jaminyjarti in Northern Aboriginal Australia', *Oceania*, vol. 84, no. 1, 2014, pp. 43–4.

p. 130 New South Wales Aboriginal Land Council, 'End Prosecutions for Aboriginal Cultural Fishing: Media Release', 20 October 2021: alc.org.au/newsroom/media-releases/end-prosecutions-for-aboriginal-cultural-fishing/ (accessed 24 April 2023).

p. 131 Tanya J. King, Rachel Turner, Vincent Versace, Kirsten Abernethy, Sue Kilpatrick and Susan Brumby, 'Mental Health in the Commercial Fishing Industry: Modern Uncertainties and Traditional Risks', *Fish and Fisheries*, vol. 22, no. 5, 2021, pp. 1136–49.

Conclusion

p. 133 Daniel Montoya and Emily Ravlich, 'Murray–Darling Basin: Fish Kills and Current Conditions', *Issues Backgrounder*, no. 2, NSW Parliamentary Research Service, 2019.

p. 134 Charles Sturt, *Two Expeditions into the Interior of Southern Australia During the Years 1828, 1829, 1830, 1831: With Observations on the Soil, Climate, and General Resources of the Colony of New South Wales*, Sydney: University of Sydney Library, 2001, p. 99.

p. 134 L. M. van Eeden et al., 'Impacts of the Unprecedented 2019–2020 Bushfires on Australian Animals: Report Prepared for WWF-Australia', Ultimo, NSW: WWF-Australia, 2020.

p. 134 Graham Readfearn, 'UNESCO Recommends Great Barrier Reef World Heritage Site Should Be Listed as "In Danger"', *Guardian*, 22 June 2021.

p. 135 Anne Jacobsen, 'Steam Trawling on the South-east Continental Shelf of Australia: An Environmental History of Fishing, Management and Science in NSW, 1865–1961', PhD thesis, School of Geography and Environmental Studies, University of Tasmania, 2010, p. 1; Callum Roberts, *The Unnatural History of the Sea*, Washington, DC: Island Press/Shearwater Books, 2007, p. 336; Caroline Ford, *Sydney Beaches: A History*, Sydney: NewSouth Publishing, 2014, pp. 226–37; Russell G. Richards et al., 'Effects and Mitigations of Ocean Acidification on Wild and Aquaculture Scallop and Prawn Fisheries in Queensland, Australia', *Fisheries Research*, vol. 161, 2015, pp. 42–56; Ana Norman Lopez et al., 'Linking Physiological, Population and Socio-economic Assessments of Climate-Change Impacts on Fisheries', *Fisheries Research*, vol. 148, 2013, pp. 18–26.

p. 135 John R. Ford and Paul Hamer, 'The Forgotten Shellfish Reefs of Coastal Victoria: Documenting the Loss of a Marine Ecosystem over 200 Years since European Settlement', *Proceedings of the Royal Society of Victoria*, vol. 128, no. 1, 2016, p. 87; Chris L. Gillies et al., 'Australian Shellfish Ecosystems: Past Distribution, Current Status and Future Direction', *PLOS ONE*, vol. 13, no. 2, 2018, pp. 1–23; Michael W. Beck et al., 'Oyster Reefs at Risk and Recommendations for Conservation, Restoration, and Management', *BioScience*, vol. 61, no. 2, 2011, pp. 107–16.

Endnotes

p. 136 Ford, *Sydney Beaches*, pp. 226–37.

p. 136 Tom Griffiths, 'The Planet is Alive: Radical Histories for Uncanny Times', *Griffith Review*, no. 20, 2019, pp. 61–72.

pp. 136–7 Heidi K. Alleway and Sean D. Connell, 'Loss of an Ecological Baseline Through the Eradication of Oyster Reefs from Coastal Ecosystems and Human Memory', *Conservation Biology*, vol. 29, no. 3, p. 803.

p. 137 Daniel Pauly, 'Anecdotes and the Shifting Baseline Syndrome of Fisheries', *Trends in Ecology and Evolution*, vol. 10, no. 10, 1995, p. 430; Andrea Gaynor and Joy McCann, '"I've Had Dolphins . . . Looking for Abalone for Me": Oral History and the Subjectivities of Marine Engagement', *The Oral History Review*, vol. 44, no. 2, 2017, pp. 260–77.

p. 137 Gaynor and McCann, '"I've Had Dolphins . . . Looking for Abalone for Me"', pp. 260–77.

p. 137 Kristin Kleisner et al., 'Australia: Reconstructing Estimates of Total Fisheries Removal, 1950–2010', *Working Paper Series*, Fisheries Centre, University of British Columbia, 2015, p. 6; Roberts, *The Unnatural History of the Sea*, p. 338; Noel Haysom, *Trawlers, Trollers and Trepangers: The Story of the Queensland Commercial Fishing Industry pre-1988*, Brisbane: QLD Department of Primary Industries, 2001, p. 59; Kieren Kelleher, 'Discards in the World's Marine Fisheries: An Update', FAO Fisheries Technical Paper, no. 470, 2004.

pp. 137–8 Kleisner et al., 'Australia: Reconstructing Estimates of Total Fisheries Removal', p. 13; L. D. West, K. E. Stark, J. J. Murphy, J. M. Lyle and F. A. Ochwada-Doyle, 'Survey of Recreational Fishing in New South Wales and the ACT, 2013/14', *Fisheries Final Report Series*, no. 149, NSW DPI, 2015.

p. 138 Adrian Medder, 'Is Aquaculture Sustainable?', Australian Marine Conservation Society: marineconservation.org.au/is-aquaculture-sustainable/ (accessed 13 April 2023).

pp. 138–9 'Sand Flathead, the Most Popular Fish for Tasmanian Anglers, Now at "Depleted" Status', *ABC News*, Australian Broadcasting Corporation, 22 December 2022; J. Hughes and M. J. Stewart, 'NSW Stock Status Summary 2018/19 – Yellowtail Kingfish (*Seriola Ialandi*)', NSW Department of Primary Industries: Fisheries NSW, 2020: dpi.nsw.gov.

171

au/__data/assets/pdf_file/0010/1329571/stock-status-summary-2021-yellowtail-kingfish.pdf (accessed 26 April 2023); J. Hughes, 'NSW Stock Status Summary 2018/19 – Mulloway (*Argyrosomus japonicus*)', NSW Department of Primary Industries: Fisheries NSW, 2020; dpi.nsw.gov.au/__data/assets/pdf_file/0005/1329611/stock-status-summary-2021-mulloway.pdf (accessed 26 April 2023).

p. 139 H. Patterson, D. Bromhead, D. Galeano, J. Larcombe, T. Timmiss, J. Woodhams and R. Curtotti, 'Fishery Status Reports 2022', Canberra: Australian Bureau of Agricultural and Resource Economics and Sciences, 2022, p. 6.

p. 139 Paul Toohey, 'Catch Cry', *The Bulletin*, 18 January 2005, p. 45; Roberts, *The Unnatural History of the Sea*, p. 336; John Wilkinson, 'Commercial Fishing in NSW: Origins and Developments to the Early 1990s', Sydney: NSW Parliamentary Library Research Service, 1997, p. 49.

p. 139 Food and Agriculture Organization of the United Nations, *The State of World Fisheries and Aquaculture 2022. Towards Blue Transformation*, Rome: FAO, 2022; Jacobsen, 'Steam Trawling on the South-east Continental Shelf of Australia', p. 1.

p. 141 Ford and Hamer, 'The Forgotten Shellfish Reefs of Coastal Victoria', p. 87; Gillies et al., 'Australian Shellfish Ecosystems', pp. 1–23; Beck et al., 'Oyster Reefs at Risk', pp. 107–16.

p. 141 Y. M. Tan et al., 'Seagrass Restoration is Possible: Insights and Lessons from Australia and New Zealand', *Frontiers in Marine Science*, vol. 7, 2020, pp. 1–21; Lorna Howlett et al., 'Adoption of Coral Propagation and Out-planting via the Tourism Industry to Advance Site Stewardship on the Northern Great Barrier Reef', *Ocean & Coastal Management*, vol. 225, no. 10, 2022, pp. 1–13.

p. 141 See, for example, the work of OzFish Unlimited: ozfish.org.au (accessed 24 April 2023).

BIBLIOGRAPHY

'A Fishing Party's Experience', *The Chronicle* (Adelaide), 14 March 1903, p. 39.

'A Piscatorial Pleasure Party', *Illustrated Sydney News and New South Wales Agriculturalist and Grazier*, 31 March 1876, p. 15.

'A Western Tourist Centre', *Sydney Morning Herald*, 31 October 1905, p. 6.

'Aboriginal People Living and Working on the NSW Coast: A Historical Review', Sydney: Office of Environment and Heritage NSW, 2012.

'Aboriginal Women's Heritage: Port Stephens', Sydney: Department of Environment and Conservation NSW, 2004.

'Amateur Fishermen's Association of New South Wales', *Sydney Morning Herald*, 20 February 1895, p. 5.

'An Act to Regulate Oyster Fisheries and to Encourage the Formation of Oyster-beds, 1st February, 1868'; legislation.nsw.gov.au/view/pdf/asmade/act-1868-3a (accessed 13 April 2023).

'Anglers Slam Labor over Sydney Lock-outs', *Fishing World Magazine*, 2 October 2014; fishingworld.com.au/news/anglers-slam-labor-over-sydney-lock-outs (accessed 13 April 2023).

'Australia Seeks Right of Coastal States to Establish Fishery Zones', *Australian Fisheries*, vol. 30, no. 9, 1971, pp. 9–11.

'Big Tuna: The Problem of Where They Go', *Australian Fisheries*, vol. 1, no. 1, 1941–2, p. 3.

'Filleting Machine Developed', *Australian Fisheries*, vol. 29, no. 9, 1970, p. 27.

'Fishing', *The Yeoman, and Australian Acclimatiser*, 5 September 1863, p. 774.

'N.S.W. Scientist to Study Anglers' Problems', *Australian Fisheries*, vol. 30, no. 12, 1971, p. 2.

'Nature and Leisure', *The Australian Rod & Gun*, vol. 3, no. 3, 1950, p. 19.

'Northern Territory Barramundi Fishery Environmental Management System', Darwin: Northern Territory Seafood Council, 2010.

'Oyster Fisheries', *The Sydney Mail and New South Wales Advertiser*, 9 September 1871, p. 893.

Report of the Royal Commission Appointed on the 8th January, to Inquire into and Report on the Fisheries of this Colony, Sydney: Thomas Richards, Government Printer, 1880.

'Sand Flathead, the Most Popular Fish for Tasmanian Anglers, Now at "Depleted" Status', *ABC News*, Australian Broadcasting Corporation, 22 December 2022.

'The Australian Herring', *The Shoalhaven Telegraph*, 11 July 1896, p. 2.

'The Jaws of Death', *The Australian Angler*, vol. 1, no. 1, 1969, pp. 12–15, 49.

'Turning Turtle into Canned Delicacies', *The Daily News*, 11 October 1923, p. 11.

'Turtle Products', *The West Australian*, 10 October 1923, p. 7.

'Ulladulla Fishermen See Troubled Waters Ahead', *Australian Fisheries*, vol. 49, no. 4, 1990, pp. 22–4.

Adams, Sid, 'Southern Bluefin Tuna: A Contested History', in J. Christensen and M. Tull (eds), *Historical Perspectives of Fisheries Exploitation in the Indo-Pacific*, New York: Springer, 2006, pp. 173–90.

Aflalo, Frederick G., *Sea-fish: An Account of the Methods of Angling as Practised on the English Coast, with Notes on the Capture of the more Sporting Fishes in Continental, South African, and Australian Waters*, London: George Routledge and Sons, c. 1904.

—, *A Sketch of the Natural History of Australia: With Some Notes on Sport*, London: MacMillan and Co., 1896.

Alleway, Heidi K. and Sean D. Connell, 'Loss of an Ecological Baseline Through the Eradication of Oyster Reefs from Coastal Ecosystems and Human Memory', *Conservation Biology*, vol. 29, no. 3, pp. 795–804.

Ashby, K. C. G., 'Apathetic Anglers', *Australian Sportfishing*, vol. 1, no. 4, 1969, p. 67.

Attenbrow, Val, *Sydney's Aboriginal Past*, Sydney: UNSW Press, 2010.

Bibliography

Australian Fisheries Management Authority, 'Gemfish' (2023); afma.gov. au/species/gemfish#referenced-section-1 (accessed 13 April 2023).

Australian Marine Parks, 'Impact of Aquaculture', National Oceans Office, 2001.

Australian Museum, 'Aboriginal People of Coastal Sydney: Place Names Chart'; australianmuseum.net.au/place-names-chart (accessed 13 April 2023).

Baelde, Pascale, 'Fishers' Description of Changes in Fishing Gear and Fishing Practices in the Australian South East Trawl Fishery', *Marine & Freshwater Research*, vol. 52, no. 4, 2001, pp. 411–17.

Baker, Elizabeth, 'Recreational Fishers in Australia: A Social Snapshot', Ballina, NSW: OzFish Unlimited, 2017; ozfish.org.au/wp-content/ uploads/2017/05/Recreational-Fishers-in-Australia-a-social-snapshot-sml.pdf (accessed 24 April 2023).

Barber, Kim and Hilary Rumley, 'Gunanurang: (Kununurra) Big River Aboriginal Cultural Values of the Ord River and Wetlands', Perth: The Water and Rivers Commission, WA, 2003.

Barnes, Jillian, 'Aboriginal Cultural Tourism: Enterprise, Contested Mobilities and Negotiating a Responsible Australian Travel Culture', *Journal of Australian Indigenous Issues*, vol. 18, no. 1, 2015, pp. 116–42.

Beck, Michael W. et al., 'Oyster Reefs at Risk and Recommendations for Conservation, Restoration, and Management', *BioScience*, vol. 61, no. 2, 2011, pp. 107–16.

Bodkin, Frances, *D'harawal Seasons and Climate Cycles*, Sydney: F. Bodkin and L. Robertson, 2008.

Bowen, Alistair, 'Material Evidence for Early Commercial Fishing Activities on the Far South Coast of New South Wales', *Australasian Historical Archaeology*, vol. 22, 2004, pp. 79–89.

—, 'Dating a Chinese Fish Curing Camp at Port Albert, Victoria', *The Artefact*, vol. 30, 2007, pp. 4–30.

—, 'The Central Role of Chinese People in Australia's Colonial Fishing Industry', *Journal of Australian Colonial History*, vol. 12, 2010, pp. 97–118.

Bradley, William, Journal titled 'A Voyage to New South Wales', December 1786–May 1792, Mitchell Library, State Library of New South Wales, 1802; acms.sl.nsw.gov.au/_transcript/2015/D02131/a138.html (accessed 13 April 2023).

Brennan, Claire, 'Imperial Game: A History of Hunting, Society, Exotic Species and the Environment in New Zealand and Victoria 1840–1901', PhD thesis, Department of History, University of Melbourne, 2004.

Cadzow, Alison et al., *Waterborne: Vietnamese Australians and Sydney's Georges River Parks and Green Spaces*, Sydney: UTS ePress, 2011.

Cameron, John, *The Fisherman: A Guide to the Inexperienced: How, When and Where to Catch Fish*, Brisbane: Gordon & Gotch, 1888.

Cathcart, Michael, *Starvation in a Land of Plenty*, Canberra: NLA Publishing, 2013.

CCSBT Extended Scientific Committee, 'Report on Biology, Stock Status and Management of Southern Bluefin Tuna: 2022', Canberra: Commission for the Conservation of Southern Bluefin Tuna, 2022; ccsbt.org/sites/default/files/userfiles/file/docs_english/meetings/meeting_reports/ccsbt_29/ESC27_Attachment_07_ReportOnBiology StatusManagement.pdf (accessed 4 April 2023).

Christensen, Joseph and Gary Jackson, 'Shark Bay Snapper: Science, Policy, and the Decline of and Recovery of a Marine Recreational Fishery', in J. Christensen and M. Tull (eds), *Historical Perspectives of Fisheries Exploitation in the Indo-Pacific*, New York: Springer, 2006, pp. 251–68.

Clark, John Heaviside, *Field Sports &c. &c. of the Native Inhabitants of New South Wales: With Ten Plates by the Author*, London: Edward Orme, 1813.

Clark, Ralph, *The Journal and Letters of Lt Ralph Clark 1787 – 1792*, Sydney: University of Sydney Library, 1981.

Clarke, John, *Old Salt*, Sydney: Royal Australian Historical Society, 2011.

Clayton, A. M., *New South Wales Rod Fishers' Society: The First 75 Years*, Sydney: The Society, 1978.

Clifford, Pat, 'Australian Fishing Industry – Interviews with New South Wales Fishermen', State Library of New South Wales, MLOH 277/9, 1990.

Clode, Danielle, *Killers in Eden: The True Story of Killer Whales and their Remarkable Partnership with the Whalers of Twofold Bay*, Crows Nest, NSW: Allen & Unwin, 2002.

Colhoun, Eric A. and Adrian Piper, 'Stone Fish Traps at Cooks Corner, Freycinet Peninsula, Eastern Tasmania', *Australian Archaeology*, vol. 14, 1982, pp. 115–18.

Collins, Ben, 'Reconciling the Dark History of Slavery and Murder in

Bibliography

Australian Pearling, Points to a Brighter Future', *ABC News*, Australian Broadcasting Corporation, 9 September 2018.

Collins, David, *An Account of the English Colony in New South Wales With Remarks on the Dispositions, Customs, Manners, &c., of the Native Inhabitants of that Country. To which are Added, Some Particulars of New Zealand*, London: T. Cadell, jun. and W. Davies, 1798.

—, *An Account of the English Colony in New South Wales, From Its First Settlement in January 1788, to August 1801: With Remarks on the Dispositions, Customs, Manners, &c. of the Native Inhabitants of That Country* (2nd ed.), London: T. Cadell, jun. and W. Davies, 1804.

Cook, James, *Journal of H.M.S. Endeavour, 1768–1771*, MS 1, National Library of Australia.

Cruse, Beryl, Liddy Stewart and Sue Norman, *Mutton Fish*, Canberra: Aboriginal Studies Press, 2005.

Daley, Ben et al., 'Exploiting Marine Wildlife in Queensland: The Commercial Dugong and Marine Turtle Fisheries, 1847–1969', *Australian Economic History Review*, vol. 48, no. 3, 2008, pp. 227–65.

Dann, John C. (ed.), *The Nagle Journal: A Diary of the Life of Jacob Nagle, Sailor, from the Year 1775 to 1841*, New York: Weidenfeld & Nicolson, c. 1988.

Dannevig, Harald, *Fisheries: Notes on Australia's Fisheries with a Summary of the Results Obtained by the F.I.S. 'Endeavour'*, Melbourne: Department of Trade and Customs, 1913.

Dargin, Peter, *Aboriginal Fisheries of the Darling–Barwon Rivers*, Brewarrina, NSW: Brewarrina Historical Society, 1976.

de Freycinet, Louis, *Voyage autour du monde entrepris par ordre du Roi . . . exécuté sur les corvettes de S. M. l'Uranie et la Physicienne, pendant les années 1817, 1818, 1819 et 1820, historique, tome deuxième – deuxième partie*, Paris: Chez Pillet Aîné, 1839.

Drummond, Sarah, *Salt Story: Of Sea-Dogs and Fisherwomen*, Fremantle: Fremantle Press, 2014.

Dunlop, E. W., 'John Joseph Oxley', *Australian Dictionary of Biography*; adb.anu.edu.au/biography/oxley-john-joseph-2530 (accessed 13 April 2023).

Dunn, Bob, *Angling in Australia: Its History and Writings*, Balmain, NSW: David Ell Press, 1991.

Egloff, Brian, *Wreck Bay: An Aboriginal Fishing Community*, Canberra: Aboriginal Studies Press, 1990.

Ferris, Lance, 'Fishing's Poisoned Barb', *Australian Geographic*, vol. 74, 2004, p. 32.

First Fleet Fellowship Victoria Inc., 'List of Livestock and Provisions'; firstfleetfellowship.org.au/library/first-fleetlist-livestock-provisions-plants-seeds/ (accessed 13 April 2023).

Fisheries Research and Development Corporation, 'National Recreational Fishing Survey: update', 2022; frdc.com.au/about-recreational-fishing/nrfs (accessed 31 March 2023).

Fitzsimmons, Caitlin, '"If It All Goes Wrong, I'd Rather Be on the Water": Covid-19 Sparks Boating Boom', *Sydney Morning Herald*, 17 January 2021.

Flood, Josephine, *The Original Australians: The Story of the Aboriginal People*, Sydney: Allen & Unwin, 2019.

Food and Agriculture Organization of the United Nations, *The State of World Fisheries and Aquaculture 2022. Towards Blue Transformation*, Rome: FAO, 2022.

Ford, Caroline, *Sydney Beaches: A History*, Sydney: NewSouth Publishing, 2014.

Ford, John R. and Paul Hamer, 'The Forgotten Shellfish Reefs of Coastal Victoria: Documenting the Loss of a Marine Ecosystem over 200 Years since European Settlement', *Proceedings of the Royal Society of Victoria*, vol. 128, no. 1, 2016, pp. 87–105.

Franklin, Adrian, 'Performing Acclimatisation: The Agency of Trout Fishing in Postcolonial Australia', *Ethnos*, vol. 76, no. 1, 2011, pp. 19–40.

Frawley, Jodi, 'Kissing Fish: Rex Hunt, Popular Culture, Sustainability and Fishing Practices', *Journal of Australian Studies*, vol. 39, no. 3, 2015, pp. 307–25.

Frawley, Jodi, Scott Nichols, Heather Goodall and Liz Baker, *Talking Fish: Making Connections with the Rivers of the Murray Darling Basin*, Canberra: Murray Darling Basin Authority, 2012.

Ganter, Regina, 'Muslim Australians: The Deep Histories of Contact', *Journal of Australian Studies*, vol. 32, no. 4, 2008, pp. 481–92.

Gapps, Stephen, 'Finding Bloody Point', *The Sydney Wars*, 11 March 2019; the sydneywars.com/2019/03/11/finding-bloody-point/ (accessed 3 April 2023).

—, *The Sydney Wars*, Sydney: NewSouth Publishing, 2018.

Garner, Bill, *Born in a Tent: How Camping Makes Us Australian*, Sydney: NewSouth Publishing, 2013.

Bibliography

Gaynor, Andrea, 'Shifting Baselines or Shifting Currents? An Environmental History of Fish and Fishing in the South-west Capes Region of Western Australia', in J. Christensen and M. Tull (eds), *Historical Perspectives of Fisheries Exploitation in the Indo-Pacific*, New York: Springer, 2006, pp. 231–50.

Gaynor, Andrea and Joy McCann, '"I've Had Dolphins ... Looking for Abalone for Me": Oral History and the Subjectivities of Marine Engagement', *The Oral History Review*, vol. 44, no. 2, 2017, pp. 260–77.

Gibson, Peter (ed.), *The Flowing Stream: 100 Years of Angling with the New South Wales Rod Fishers' Society*, Paddington, NSW: Creek of Peace, 2004.

Gillies, Chris L. et al., 'Australian Shellfish Ecosystems: Past Distribution, Current Status and Future Direction', *PLOS ONE*, vol. 13, no. 2, 2018, pp. 1–23.

Gilmore, Mary, *Old Days – Old Ways*, Sydney: Angus and Robertson, 1963.

Gowers, Richard J., 'Selling the "Untold Wealth" in the Seas: A Social and Cultural History of the South-east Australian Shelf Trawling Industry, 1915–1961', *Environment and History*, vol. 14, no. 2, 2000, pp. 266–75.

Grieve, Chris and Geoff Richard, 'Recent History of Australia's South East Fishery: A Manager's Perspective', *Marine & Freshwater Research*, vol. 52, 2001, pp. 377–86.

Griffiths, Billy, *Deep Time Dreaming: Uncovering Ancient Australia*, Carlton, Vic: Black Inc, 2018.

Griffiths, Shane P., Joanne Bryant, Henry F. Raymond and Peter A. Newcombe, 'Quantifying Subjective Human Dimensions of Recreational Fishing: Does Good Health Come to Those Who Bait?', *Fish and Fisheries*, vol. 18, no. 1, 2017, pp. 171–84.

Griffiths, Tom, 'The Planet is Alive: Radical Histories for Uncanny Times', *Griffith Review*, no. 20, 2019, pp. 61–72.

Hale, Pamela and Paul Ashton, *Raising the Nation: A History of Commonwealth Departments of Agriculture, Fisheries and Forestry, 1901-2001*, Canberra: Department of Agriculture, Forestry and Fisheries, 2002.

Halkyard, Brooke, 'Exploiting Green and Hawksbill Turtles in Western Australia: The Commercial Marine Turtle Fishery', in J. Christensen and M. Tull (eds), *Historical Perspectives of Fisheries Exploitation in the Indo-Pacific*, New York: Springer, 2006, pp. 211–30.

Hardy, Wal, 'The Xmas Angle', *Australian Outdoors & Fishing*, vol. 14, no. 2, 1955, p. 31.

Harris, David, "'It's just fly fishing against net fishing . . .'": Commercial Fishing, Angling and the Gippsland Lakes, 1870s, 1880s', in E. Eklund and J. Fenley (eds), *Earth and Industry: Stories from Gippsland*, Melbourne: Monash University Press, 2015, pp. 124–45.

Harrison, Anthony J., 'The Fisheries Savant: William Saville-Kent in Victoria, 1887–8', *Historical Records of Australian Science*, vol. 11, no. 3, 1997, pp. 419–29.

Haysom, Noel, *Trawlers, Trollers and Trepangers: The Story of the Queensland Commercial Fishing Industry pre-1988*, Brisbane: QLD Department of Primary Industries, 2001.

Hedge, John, *Trout Fishing in New South Wales*, Sydney: Abbey Publishing Co., 1962.

Henry, Gary W. and Jeremy M. Lyle, *The National Recreational and Indigenous Fishing Survey*, Canberra: Australian Government Department of Agriculture, Fisheries and Forestry, 2003.

Hiscock, Peter, *Archaeology of Ancient Australia*, London & New York: Routledge, 2008.

Hooker, Joseph (ed.), *Journal of the Right Hon. Sir Joseph Banks . . . During Captain Cook's First Voyage in* H.M.S. Endeavour *in 1768–71 to Terra del Fuego, Otahite, New Zealand, Australia, the Dutch East Indies, etc.*, London: Macmillan & Co., Ltd, 1896.

Hoskins, Ian, *Coast*, Sydney: NewSouth Publishing, 2013.

Howlett, Lorna et al., 'Adoption of Coral Propagation and Out-planting via the Tourism Industry to Advance Site Stewardship on the Northern Great Barrier Reef', *Ocean & Coastal Management*, vol. 225, no. 10, 2022, pp. 1–13.

Hughes, J., 'NSW Stock Status Summary 2018/19 – Mulloway (*Argyrosomus japonicus*)', NSW Department of Primary Industries: Fisheries NSW, 2020; dpi.nsw.gov.au/__data/assets/pdf_file/0005/1329611/stock-status-summary-2021-mulloway.pdf (accessed 26 April 2023).

Hughes, J. and M. J. Stewart, 'NSW Stock Status Summary 2018/19 – Yellowtail Kingfish (*Seriola Ialandi*)', NSW Department of Primary Industries: Fisheries NSW, 2020; dpi.nsw.gov.au/__data/assets/pdf_file/0010/1329571/stock-status-summary-2021-yellowtail-kingfish.pdf (accessed 26 April 2023).

Hughes, Robert, *A Jerk on One End: Reflections of a Mediocre Fisherman*, London: Harvill Press, 1999.

Bibliography

Hunt, Janet, 'The NSW Government Needs to Stop Prosecuting Aboriginal Fishers if it Really Wants to Close the Gap', *The Conversation*, 11 October 2021; theconversation.com/the-nsw-government-needs-to-stop-prosecuting-aboriginal-fishers-if-it-really-wants-to-close-the-gap-168749 (accessed 2 February 2023).

Isaacs, Nigel, 'Sydney's First Ice', *Dictionary of Sydney*, 2011; dictionaryof sydney.org/entry/sydneys_first_ice (access 13 April 2023).

Jacobsen, Anne, 'Steam Trawling on the South-east Continental Shelf of Australia: An Environmental History of Fishing, Management and Science in NSW, 1865–1961', PhD thesis, School of Geography and Environmental Studies, University of Tasmania, 2010.

James, Anthony, 'I Remember the Day', *The Australian Angler*, vol. 1, no. 12, 1971, pp. 18–19, 40.

Jones, Rhys, 'The Tasmanian Paradox', in R. V. S. Wright (ed.), *Stone Tools as Cultural Markers: Change, Evolution and Complexity*, Canberra: Australian Institute of Aboriginal Studies, 1977, pp. 189–204.

Karskens, Grace, 'Barangaroo and the Eora Fisherwomen', *Dictionary of Sydney*; dictionaryofsydney.org/entry/barangaroo_and_the_eora_fisher-women (accessed 26 April 2023).

— *The Colony: A History of Early Sydney*, Crows Nest, NSW: Allen & Unwin, 2009.

Kelleher, Kieren, 'Discards in the World's Marine Fisheries: An Update', FAO Fisheries Technical Paper, no. 470, 2004.

Kerr, Garry, *Craft and Craftsmen of Australian Fishing 1870–1970*, Portland: Mains'l Books, 1985.

King, Tanya J., Rachel Turner, Vincent Versace, Kirsten Abernethy, Sue Kilpatrick and Susan Brumby, 'Mental Health in the Commercial Fishing Industry: Modern Uncertainties and Traditional Risks', *Fish and Fisheries*, vol. 22, no. 5, 2021, pp. 1136–49.

Klaer, N. L., 'Steam Trawl Catches from South-eastern Australia from 1918 to 1957: Trends in Catch Rates and Species Composition', *Marine and Freshwater Research*, vol. 52, no. 4, 2001, pp. 399–410.

Kleisner, Kristin et al., 'Australia: Reconstructing Estimates of Total Fisheries Removal, 1950–2010', *Working Paper Series*, Fisheries Centre, University of British Columbia, 2015.

Kurlansky, Mark, *Cod: A Biography of a Fish that Changed the World*, New York: Walker and Co., 1997.

Lawler, Susan, 'Rabbits of the River: Trout are Not Native to Australia', *The Conversation*, 13 May 2013; theconversation.com/rabbits-of-the-river-trout-are-not-native-to-australia-14115 (accessed 13 April 2023).

Leichhardt, Ludwig, *Journal of an Overland Expedition in Australia, from Moreton Bay to Port Essington, a Distance of Upwards of 3000 Miles, During the Years 1844–1845*, London: T. & W. Boone, 1847.

Lenanton, R. C. J., 'The Commercial Fisheries of Temperate Western Australian Estuaries: Early Settlement to 1975', North Beach, WA: Western Australian Marine Research Laboratories, Department of Fisheries and Wildlife, 1984.

Little, John, *Down to the Sea: The True Saga of an Australian Fishing Dynasty*, Sydney: MacMillan, 2004.

Macknight, Campbell, '"The view from Marege": Australian Knowledge of Makassar and the Impact of the Trepang Industry Across Two Centuries', *Aboriginal History*, vol. 35, 2011, pp. 127–38.

Malseed, B. E. and N. R. Sumner, 'A 12-month Survey of Recreational Fishing in the Swan-Canning Estuary Basin of Western Australia during 1998–99', *Fisheries Research Report*, no. 126, Perth: WA Marine Research Laboratories, Fisheries Research Division, 2001.

Martin, David, 'Northern Territory Fishing History Traced', *Feedstuffs*, vol. 72, no. 5, 2000, p. 13.

—, 'Northern Territory Fisheries Expanding', *Feedstuffs*, vol. 72, no. 5, 2000, p. 12.

Martin, Sarah, Hubert Chanson, Badger Bates, Duncan Keenan-Jones and Michael C. Westaway, 'Indigenous Fish Traps and Fish Weirs on the Darling (Baaka) River, South-eastern Australia, and their Influence on the Ecology and Morphology of the River and Floodplains', *Archaeology in Oceania*, 2022, pp. 1–24.

Mathews, R. H., 'The Aboriginal Fisheries at Brewarrina', *Journal and Proceedings of the Royal Society of New South Wales*, vol. 37, 1903, pp. 146–56.

McGhie, Michael, 'Fishing the Peel-Harvey Estuary', *Friends of Mandurah Community Museum Newsletter*, October 2010, pp. 1–5.

McNiven, Ian, 'Saltwater People: Spiritscapes, Maritime Rituals and the Archaeology of Australian Indigenous Seascapes', *World Archaeology*, vol. 35, no. 3, 2004, pp. 329–49.

McNiven, Ian, Joe Crouch, Thomas Richards, Kale Sniderman, Nic Dolby

Bibliography

and Gunditj Mirring, 'Phased Redevelopment of an Ancient Gunditjmara Fish Trap over the Past 800 Years: Muldoons Trap Complex, Lake Condah, Southwestern Victoria', *Australian Archaeology*, vol. 81, no. 1, 2015, pp. 44–58.

McPhee, D. P. et al., 'Swallowing the Bait: Is Recreational Fishing in Australia Ecologically Sustainable?', *Pacific Conservation Biology*, vol. 8, 2004, pp. 40–51.

Medder, Adrian, 'Is Aquaculture Sustainable?', Australian Marine Conservation Society; marineconservation.org.au/is-aquaculture-sustainable/ (accessed 13 April 2023).

Minard, Peter, 'Salmonid Acclimatisation in Colonial Victoria: Improvement, Restoration and Recreation 1858–1909', *Environment and History*, vol. 21, no. 2, 2015, pp. 179–99.

Mitchell, Thomas, *Three Expeditions into the Interior of Eastern Australia* (vol. 1), London: T. & W Boone, 1838.

Momtaz, Salim and William Gladstone, 'Ban on Commercial Fishing in the Estuarine Waters of New South Wales, Australia: Community Consultation and Social Impacts', *Environmental Impact Assessment Review*, vol. 28, no. 2–3, 2008, pp. 214–25.

Montoya, Daniel and Emily Ravlich, 'Murray Darling Basin: Fish Kills and Current Conditions', *Issues Backgrounder*, no. 2, NSW Parliamentary Research Service, 2019.

Mulvaney, D. J. and Johan Kamminga, *Prehistory of Australia*, Washington D.C.: Smithsonian Institution Press, 1999.

Murgatroyd, Sarah, *The Dig Tree: The Story of Burke and Wills*, Melbourne: Text Publishing, 2012.

New South Wales Aboriginal Land Council, 'End Prosecutions for Aboriginal Cultural Fishing: Media Release', 20 October 2021; alc.org.au/newsroom/media-releases/end-prosecutions-for-aboriginal-cultural-fishing/ (accessed 24 April 2023).

Newton, John, *A Savage History of Whaling in the Pacific and Southern Oceans*, Sydney: NewSouth Publishing, 2013.

Nicols, Arthur, *Acclimatisation of the Salmonidae at the Antipodes: Its History and Results*, London: Sampson Low, Marston Searle & Rivington, 1882.

Noble, W. G., 'Murray Cod' (letter to the editor), *Sydney Morning Herald*, 6 October 1955, p. 2.

Noblet, E. M., *The Winds that Blew at Cossack*, Sydney: Angus & Robertson, 1968.

Norman-Lopez, Ana et al., 'Linking Physiological, Population and Socio-economic Assessments of Climate-Change Impacts on Fisheries', *Fisheries Research*, vol. 148, 2013, pp. 18–26.

Oxley, John, *Journals of Two Expeditions into the Interior of New South Wales Undertaken by Order of the British Government in the Years 1817–18*, Sydney: University of Sydney Library, 2002.

Palmer, Lisa, 'Fishing Lifestyles: "Territorians", Traditional Owners and the Management of Recreational Fishing in Kakadu National Park', *Australian Geographical Studies*, vol. 42, no. 1, 2004, p. 71.

Pascoe, Bruce, *Dark Emu: Black Seeds – Agriculture or Accident?*, Broome, WA: Magabala Books, 2014.

Paterson, G., *The History of New South Wales: From its First Discovery to the Present Time*, Newcastle-upon-Tyne: MacKenzie and Dent, 1811.

Patterson, H., D. Bromhead, D. Galeano, J. Larcombe, T. Timmiss, J. Woodhams and R. Curtotti, 'Fishery Status Reports 2022', Canberra: Australian Bureau of Agricultural and Resource Economics and Sciences, 2022.

Pauly, Daniel, 'Anecdotes and the Shifting Baseline Syndrome of Fisheries', *Trends in Ecology and Evolution*, vol. 10, no. 10, 1995, p. 430.

—, *Darwin's Fishes: An Encyclopedia of Ichthyology, Ecology, and Evolution*, Cambridge: Cambridge University Press, 2007.

Pepperell, J. G., 'The Good Old Days? Historical Insights into Coastal NSW Fish Populations and their Fisheries', Sydney, The NSW Recreational Fishing Trusts Expenditure Committee, N.D.

Phillip, Arthur, *The Voyage of Governor Phillip to Botany Bay: With an Account of the Establishment of the Colonies of Port Jackson and Norfolk Island*, Sydney: University of Sydney Library, 2003.

Prayaga, Prabha et al., 'The Value of Recreational Fishing in the Great Barrier Reef, Australia: A Pooled Revealed Preference and Contingent Behaviour Model', *Marine Policy*, vol. 34, no. 2, 2010, pp. 244–51.

Puglisi, Michael and Natalina Puglisi, *Harvesting the Sea: The Story of the Puglisi Family, Fishing Pioneers*, Gordon, NSW: Mini-Publishing, 2009.

Raadik, Tarmo A., 'Recovery Actions for Seven Endemic and Threatened

Bibliography

Victorian Galaxiid Species', Victoria: Department of Environment, Land, Water and Planning, 2019.

Readfearn, Graham, 'UNESCO Recommends Great Barrier Reef World Heritage Site Should Be Listed as "In Danger"', *Guardian*, 22 June 2021.

Richards, Russell G. et al., 'Effects and Mitigations of Ocean Acidification on Wild and Aquaculture Scallop and Prawn Fisheries in Queensland, Australia', *Fisheries Research*, vol. 161, 2015, pp. 42–56.

Roberts, Alex, *Aboriginal Women's Fishing in New South Wales: A Thematic History*, Sydney: Department of Environment, Climate Change and Water NSW, 2010.

Roberts, Callum, *The Unnatural History of the Sea*, Washington, DC: Island Press/Shearwater Books, 2007.

Roughley, T. C., *Fish and Fisheries of Australia*, Sydney: Angus & Robertson, 1951.

Rowland, Stuart, 'Overview of the History, Fishery, Biology and Aquaculture of Murray Cod (Maccullochella peelii peelii)', Management of Murray Cod in the Murray–Darling Basin Workshop, 3–4 June 2004, Canberra, Murray–Darling Basin Commission.

Saunders, Brian, *Discovery of Australia's Fishes: A History of Australian Ichthyology to 1930*, Canberra: CSIRO Publishing, 2014.

Saville-Kent, William, 'Oysters in Australasia–I', *Brisbane Courier*, 20 January 1891, p. 6.

Senior, William, *Travel and Trout in the Antipodes: An Angler's Sketches in Tasmania and New Zealand*, London: Chatto and Windus, 1880.

Skinner, Graeme and Jim Wafer, 'A Checklist of Colonial Era Musical Transcriptions of Australian Indigenous Songs'; sydney.edu.au/paradisec/australharmony/checklist-indigenous-music-1.php#005-2 (accessed 15 December 2022).

Smith, Bridie, 'Trout Moved Out to Give Galaxias Breathing Space', *The Age*, 9 May 2013.

Soros-Longworth & McKenzie, 'Effects of Water Borne Traffic on the Environment of the Hawkesbury River', Sydney: Department of Public Works, 1977.

Stace, Dulcie, 'Australian Fishing Industry – Interviews with New South Wales fishermen', State Library of New South Wales, MLOH 277/9, 1990.

Steffe, A. and D. Chapman, 'A Survey of Daytime Recreational Fishing During the Annual Period, March 1999 to February 2000, in Lake Macquarie', New South Wales: NSW Fisheries, 2003.

Stewart, Douglas, *Fishing Around the Monaro: A Selection from the Seven Rivers*, Canberra: Australian National University Press, 1978.

Stockton, Jim, 'Stone Wall Fish Traps in Tasmania', *Australian Archaeology*, vol. 14, 1982, pp. 107–14.

Strauss, Richard, 'The Outdoor Living Supplement: Outdoor Recreation in Post-War Sydney 1945–1975', PhD thesis, History, Macquarie University, 2007.

Sturt, Charles, *Two Expeditions into the Interior of Southern Australia During the Years 1828, 1829, 1830, 1831: With Observations on the Soil, Climate, and General Resources of the Colony of New South Wales*, Sydney: University of Sydney Library, 2001.

Tan, Y. M. et al., 'Seagrass Restoration is Possible: Insights and Lessons from Australia and New Zealand', *Frontiers in Marine Science*, vol. 7, 2020, pp. 1–21.

Taylor, Rebe, 'The Polemics of Eating Fish in Tasmania: the Historical Evidence Revisited', *Aboriginal History*, vol. 32, 2007, pp. 1–26.

Tench, Watkin, *A Complete Account of the Settlement at Port Jackson*, Sydney: University of Sydney Library, 1998.

Tenison-Woods, Julian Edmund, *Fish and Fisheries of New South Wales*, Sydney: Government Printer, 1883.

Thackeray, Charles, *The Amateur Fisherman's Guide*, Sydney: George Robertson & Co., 1895.

The Industrial Progress of New South Wales, Sydney: Thomas Richards, Government Printer, 1871.

The Voyage of Governor Phillip to Botany Bay: With an Account of the Establishment of the Colonies of Port Jackson and Norfolk Island, Sydney: University of Sydney Library, 2003.

Thomas, Martin (ed.), *Culture in Translation: The Anthropological Legacy of R. H. Mathews*, Canberra: ANU Press, 2007.

Thompson, Lindsay, *History of the Fisheries of New South Wales: With a Sketch of the Laws by which They Have Been Regulated*, Sydney: Government Printer, 1893.

Thornton-Champley, J., *Australian Angler's Guide and Sea-fisher's Manual*, Melbourne: G. Robertson, c. 1910.

Bibliography

—, *Tales of Australian Angling*, Melbourne: A.H. Massina & Co., Printers, 1912.

Thurstan, Ruth et al., 'Nineteenth Century Narratives Reveal Historic Catch Rates for Australian Snapper (*Pagrus Auratus*)', *Fish and Fisheries*, vol. 17, no. 1, pp. 1–16.

Thurstan, Ruth et al., 'Origins of the Bottom Trawling Controversy in the British Isles: 19th Century Witness Testimonies Reveal Evidence of Early Fishery Declines', *Fish and Fisheries*, vol. 15, no. 3, 2014, pp. 506–22.

Tidswell, Ken, 'Australian Fishing Industry – Interviews with New South Wales fishermen', State Library of New South Wales, MLOH 277/9, 1990.

Tilzey, R. D. J. and K. R. Rowling, 'History of Australia's South East Fishery: A Scientist's Perspective', *Marine & Freshwater Research*, vol. 52, no. 4, 2001, pp. 361–75.

Toohey, Paul, 'Catch Cry', *The Bulletin*, 18 January 2005, pp. 40–5.

Toussaint, Sandy, 'Fishing for Fish and for Jaminyjarti in Northern Aboriginal Australia', *Oceania*, vol. 84, no. 1, 2014, pp. 38–51.

Travers, Tess, 'For the Girls', *Outdoors and Fishing*, vol. 11, no. 6, 1953, p. 399.

Turnbull, John, *A Voyage Round the World In the Years 1800, 1801, 1802, 1803, and 1804, in Which the Author Visited the Principal Islands in the Pacific Ocean and the English Settlements of Port Jackson and Norfolk Island* (vol. 1.), London: Richard Phillips, 1805.

University of Wollongong, 'First Fleet Database'; firstfleet.uow.edu.au/index.html (accessed 13 April 2023).

van Eeden, L. M. et al., 'Impacts of the Unprecedented 2019–2020 Bushfires on Australian Animals: Report Prepared for WWF-Australia', Ultimo, NSW: WWF-Australia, 2020.

Voyer, Michelle, '"It's part of me": Understanding the Values, Images and Principles of Coastal Users and their Influence on the Social Acceptability of MPAs', *Marine Policy*, vol. 52, 2015, pp. 93–102.

Walker, Jean, *Origins of the Tasmanian Trout*, Hobart, Tasmania: Inland Fisheries Commission, 1988.

Wallace-Carter, Evelyn, *For They Were Fishers*, Adelaide: Amphrite Publishing House, 1987.

Walters, Ian, 'Prehistoric Fisheries in Australia: A Long and Diverse Pedigree', *Australian Fisheries*, vol. 46, no. 3, 1987, pp. 21–4.

Walton, Izaak, *The Compleat Angler or, The Contemplative Man's Recreation: Being a Discourse of Fish & Fishing not Unworthy the Perusal of Most Anglers*, New York: Hodder & Stoughton, 1911.

West, L. D., K. E. Stark, J. J. Murphy, J. M. Lyle and F. A. Ochwada-Doyle, 'Survey of Recreational Fishing in New South Wales and the ACT, 2013/14', *Fisheries Final Report Series*, no. 149, NSW DPI, 2015.

Wheelwright, Horace William, *Natural History Sketches*, London: Frederick Warne, 1871.

White, John, *Journal of a Voyage to New South Wales*, London: Debrett, 1790.

White, Richard, *The Organic Machine*, New York: Hill and Wang, c. 1995.

White, Richard, *Inventing Australia*, Sydney: George Allen and Unwin, 1981.

—, *On Holidays: A History of Getting Away in Australia*, Melbourne: Pluto Press, 2005.

Wilkinson, John, 'Commercial Fishing in NSW: Origins and Developments to the Early 1990s', Sydney: NSW Parliamentary Library Research Service, 1997.

—, 'NSW Fishing Industry: Changes and Challenges in the Twenty-First Century', NSW Parliamentary Library: Briefing Paper No 11/04, 2004.

Wills, William John (ed.), *A Successful Exploration through the Interior of Australia: From Melbourne to the Gulf of Carpentaria / from the Journals and Letters of William John Wills. Edited by His Father, William Wills*, London: Richard Bentley, 1863.

Wood, E. J. Ferguson, 'The Canning of Fish and Fish Products in Australia', *Fisheries Circular*, no. 2, 1940.

Woodford, James, 'Advance Australia Green', *Griffith Review*, vol. 19, 2008, pp. 189–93.

Worgan, George B. F. S., *Journal of a First Fleet Surgeon*, Sydney: University of Sydney Library, 2003.

Young, Matthew et al., 'Impacts of Recreational Fishing in Australia: Historical Declines, Self-regulation and Evidence of an Early Warning System', *Environmental Conservation*, vol. 41, no. 4, 2014, pp. 350–6.

ACKNOWLEDGEMENTS

This book originally came out of a serendipitous exchange between the National Library of Australia (NLA) and my agent, Jacinta di Mase, who assured Susan Hall at the NLA that she did indeed know a historian who loved fishing. I couldn't believe my luck!

As you can probably guess from the text, I'm crazy about fishing, so to have the opportunity to combine my passion with my day job was basically a dream come true. I had a lot of fun researching and writing this book – I also had a lot of help along the way. For the original publication, I'm indebted to the NLA librarians and research assistants for their generous support and archival nous, as well as John Maynard for his close reading of the book's Indigenous histories.

In this second edition, the assistance from the team at Penguin has also been amazing. I'm extremely grateful Meredith Curnow saw that this work could be re-released in a new format. When *The Catch* went out of print, I thought that might just mean a dignified, if sad, ending for the book. So I'm thrilled it now lives on with a second imprint.

Special thanks also to my editor Shané Oosthuizen, for untangling my knotty prose where necessary, and asking for elaboration and description where it had been too economical. This book is much better for her thoughtful reading.

Friends and colleagues along the way have been equally generous sharing their research and fishy tidbits. In particular, I'd like to acknowledge the assistance of the National Library of Australia, the State Library of Western Australia, the Powerhouse Museum, the Brewarrina Aboriginal Cultural Museum, the NSW Department of Primary Industries and the State Library of New South Wales (especially the indefatigable Linda Brainwood!), as well as Craig Copeland, Renee Ferene and Matt Hansen at OzFish Unlimited for their generosity in sourcing images of native fish resources. I'd also like to thank Paul Ashton, Kate Barclay, Claire Brennan, Laila Ellmoos, Caroline Ford, Jodi Frawley, Heather Goodall, Paula Hamilton, David Harris, Ian Hoskins, Tom Sear, Richard Strauss, Clare Wright and Eileen Wright. I couldn't have compiled all this research without their contributions.

Several friends also read various drafts, for which I'm truly grateful: a big shout out to Leigh Boucher, Kate Barclay, Alecia Simmonds, Sean Kelly and Dan Stacey for their engaged, constructive and thoughtful feedback and advice. Cassie McCullagh and Stephen Fitzpatrick took me on a wonderful fishing tour of Jervis Bay with the ever-generous

Acknowledgements

Jim Harnwell (who also re-read my manuscript for this second edition, and opened his amazing photographic archive for me to raid).

In particular, I'd like to thank my partner, Gab Abramowitz, and my oldest friend in the whole world, Ralph Myers, for being the best fishing companions I could ask for.

Last, but not least, I've grown up in a boisterous and extended family of fishers: thank you for your tutelage and company. This is for you.

ABOUT THE AUTHOR

In her day job, Anna Clark is a Professor of History, whose most recent book, *Making Australian History*, was longlisted for the Walkley Award and the Mark and Evette Moran Nib Literary Award. She is an internationally recognised scholar who has written extensively on historiography, history education and the role of history in everyday life. When not at her desk, Anna can be found standing with a rod on the rocks, or swimming under-water somewhere along the coast, grinning at wobbegongs, garfish and darting bream. *The Catch*, her seventh book, is the perfect marriage between her love of fish and fishing and her passion for Australian history.

Making
Australian
History

———

Anna Clark

MAKING AUSTRALIAN HISTORY

**A bold and expansive history that traces the changing
and contested project of Australia's national story.
You will think about this country differently after
reading this book.**

A few years ago Anna Clark saw a series of paintings on a sandstone
cliff face in the Northern Territory. There were characteristic
crosshatched images of fat barramundi and turtles, as well as
sprayed handprints and several human figures with spears. Next to
them was a long gun, painted with white ochre, an unmistakable
image of the colonisers. Was this an Indigenous rendering of
contact? A work of history?

Each piece of history has a message and context that depends
on who wrote it and when. Australian history has swirled and
contorted over the years: the history wars have embroiled historians,
politicians and public commentators alike, while debates over
historical fiction have been as divisive. History isn't just about
understanding what happened and why. It also reflects the
persuasions, politics and prejudices of its authors. Each iteration of
Australia's national story reveals not only the past in question, but
also the guiding concerns and perceptions of each generation of
history makers.

Making Australian History is bold and inclusive: it catalogues and
contextualises changing readings of the past, it examines the
increasingly problematic role of historians as national storytellers,
and it incorporates the stories of people.

*'Clark brings a historian's erudition to the ideas. Absolutely engrossing and it's
beautifully written.'* KATE GRENVILLE

Discover a
new favourite